MORE PHILOSOPHY OF SILVER BIRCH

MORE PHILOSOPHY OF SILVER BIRCH

Compiled by
TONY ORTZEN

The Spiritual Truth Press

First published in 1979
Reprinted 1985, 1988, 1999

This edition 2008

The Spiritual Truth Press
15 Broom Hall, Oxshott
Surrey KT22 OJZ

ISBN 978 0 85384 104 3

Printed in Great Britain by Booksprint

PREFACE

There are a number of possible reasons why you are reading this book. The first and most likely is that you are already a "follower" of Silver Birch and have found his great wisdom and spiritual insights of benefit in your life. In this case you will welcome this reprint of one of the classic books of his teachings. Maybe you have been given this book by a friend who believes its message of love, in this world and in the next, will inspire or comfort you. If so, you will not be disappointed.

Perhaps you chanced upon it on a bookshelf or saw it advertised, then curiosity got the better of you. Well, after reading its pages you may also decide that "chance" played no part in the decision and that some form of spiritual guidance has brought you and this book together.

Whatever the reason, the chances are that Silver Birch's wisdom will remain with you forever. Long after you have forgotten his precise words, his guidance will still be a very real influence whenever you need it. And if you need to jog your memory – just reach for this book and read it again. Silver Birch's words are so accessible and meaningful that you will never tire of reading them. But who is Silver Birch, the spirit guide whose words are faithfully recorded here? And who was Maurice Barbanell, the London medium who channelled that wisdom? Without an answer to these questions, many new readers – however impressed with these teachings – will be puzzled about their source.

Barbanell was the founder and editor of a weekly Spiritualist newspaper, *Psychic News*, and for half a century devoted his life to spreading spiritual knowledge through its columns and those of other publications with which he was associated. In his own obituary, which he wrote before his passsing at the age of 79 on July 17th 1981, he revealed that he was told by Estelle Roberts' Red Cloud – a spirit guide for whom he had the greatest admiration – that in a previous incarnation he had made a promise to reincarnate and devote his life to spreading Spiritualism. Though he had no knowlege of that life or promise, events certainly conspired to make it possible.

He was born to Jewish parents in a poor area of London's East End. His mother was devoutly religious but his father, a barber, was an atheist so Barbanell heard many arguments about religion during his early years. His father always won, and his son adopted the same outlook but later changed to agnosticism. Yet after hearing about Spiritualism from a speaker at a social and literary club of which he was secretary, Barbanell refused to start the debate by putting an opposing view – one of his duties – because, he explained, he had made no personal investigation and therefore his opinions were valueless. This impressed the speaker who invited Barbanell to attend a séance in which a medium, Mrs Blaustein, was entranced by various spirits of different nationalities. He was not impressed, and on a second visit fell asleep. Barbanell apologised, believing that either boredom or tiredness had been responsible, but the other circle members informed him that he had not been asleep but had been in trance and a Red Indian had spoken through him.

With the encouragement of famous Fleet Street journalist Hannen Swaffer, Barbanell founded *Psychic News* partly as a vehicle for the guide's teachings. But, because he knew he would be criticised for publishing his own mediumship in his own newspaper, Barbanell did not reveal to his readers for many years who was channelling the wisdom, by which time the guide had a huge following on his own merits.

Silver Birch spoke regularly at Barbanell's home circle and

the proceedings were always recorded in shorthand. There were a number of differences in style and procedure between Barbabell's own journalistic efforts and the way in which Silver Birch communicated, as Barbanell himself observed.

"In my working life I use words every day. I have never yet written or dictated an article with which I was satisfied when I read it. Inevitably I find, when looking at the typed material, that I can improve it by altering words, phrases and sentences. No such problem arises with the guide's teachings. These flow pefectly, requiring usually only punctuation. Another interesting aspect is the occasional use of words that I regard as arhaic and do not form part of my normal vocabulary."

But who was Silver Birch? A psychic artist depicts him as a serious-looking native American Indian with a single feather and compassionate eyes. There is evidence to suggest that this was simply a convenient persona behind which a far more spiritually evolved soul hid in order that those who read his words would judge them not by the name attached to them but by the wisdom that pervades every sentence.

Those of us who knew them both were well aware of the differences in the way they spoke and the words they used. They both had spiritual missions and they fulfilled them admirably, particularly when working together in their two-world partnership. This, as you are about to discover, has provided us with simple, uplifting, comforting and inspirational answers to the questions we all ask from time to time, about life and its purpose. They are needed now more than ever before as we prepare for the challenges which will confront us in the 21st century.

Roy Stemman
Chairman
Spiritual Truth Foundation

CONTENTS

INTRODUCTION

THIS book is the result of countless hours' reading, sifting and collation. It contains Silver Birch's views as recorded verbatim during seven years' sittings of Hannen Swaffer's home circle. Apart from the summer, they were held monthly.

I have attempted to produce a compendium of Silver Birch's philosophy and teachings as they relate to personal, national and even international affairs. The subjects chosen are deliberately diverse. Silver Birch welcomed the thorny questions from which many would prefer to shy away. In simple but profound language he paints a vocal masterpiece with an economy of words skilfully used to their full potential.

I well remember the impact this gentle spirit sage made on me during visits to the world's most famous circle. Often, I had to restrain myself from gazing at the medium. This over-energetic man, normally at the centre of a journalistic and business whirlpool, sat passively as the guide's words came. Yet to the medium it was almost anathema to sit unoccupied. Silver Birch always arrived peacefully. Since the guide first entranced his medium, then a teenage agnostic who went sceptically to a Spiritualist gathering, his philosophy has not changed.

This is not a weakness. The fact that Silver Birch's teachings have endured many world crises and social revolutions illustrate their inherent strength and practicality.

To set the stage for Silver Birch, I can do no better than to quote what he told me at one visit to his circle:

"Do not underestimate the power of the written word. Through it we have been able to reach many people in other lands. The words they have read, which I am privileged to express as an instrument for higher powers, have changed their lives and given them a course, a direction, a path they can tread. Ignorance has been replaced by knowledge, darkness by light, speculation by certainty, fear by serenity. They are able to begin to fulfil themselves, as all should who are on earth.

"All this is done by the printed word in which you are privileged to participate. It is not ephemeral, like the spoken word which is often forgotten. It is permanent. It is there to be read again and again. As understanding grows new meanings are discovered.

"Thus we are able to help many who thought no hope was possible from anything or anybody on earth. That is the great privilege of service you and I and others are able to perform. It should make us very humble and aware of the responsibility placed on us. It is to ensure that we do, say or transmit nothing that in any way would detract from the nobility, grandeur and dignity of the sublime truths we proclaim."

I can take no credit for this book and will return to the wings. Silver Birch, gentle mentor, loving guide, the stage is yours.

TONY ORTZEN

Chapter One

WHO IS SILVER BIRCH?

*WHO is Silver Birch? Why has his identity never been revealed?
Is there a reason for the guide using the astral body of a Red
Indian? These questions have been asked many times. When
two Americans visited the circle Silver Birch told them:*

I am not a Red Indian. I am using the astral body of a Red
Indian because this particular one had many psychic gifts on
earth and therefore became available for me when I was asked
to return and engage on this mission. My life on earth goes
back as an individual much further than the Red Indian I use
to speak to you.

He is just as much my medium as this medium is mine,
too. It is not possible for people like myself, who left your
world many hundreds of years ago and have achieved a certain
spiritual status, to reach you and communicate on your level
where the vibrations are entirely different. I had to have what
in your world would be a transformer, someone through whom
the vibrations can be stepped up or slowed down so that I can
achieve communication on your level.

At the same time I must maintain contact with the source
that inspires me and enables me to impart the knowledge that
I can transmit. To give you names of tribes, places and dates
would in no way establish anything that could be considered
evidential because I can obtain this information so easily.

*This produced more questions. Who was he when on earth?
How long ago was it? Silver Birch refused to be drawn,
saying:*

'I am not concerned with personalities. When it was necessary I gave conclusive evidence of my separate individuality from this medium more than once.

I do not regard it as necessary any more to say who I was on earth. If I were to give you the name of someone who was famous there is no means by which it could be proven, and it would not matter. I ask to be judged wholly and solely by what I say and try to teach on the claim that it will appeal to reason, intelligence and common sense. If I cannot win the people of your world by these methods, then I am failing.

To say I was a Pharaoh would not help. This would be merely an attempt to give myself an earthly glory which is accounted as being important in your world but not in ours. In our world the test is not your material possession, but what you did with your life.

We judge souls, not money or status. Souls matter to us. Your world has got its priorities wrong. In your own land the worship of the golden calf exceeds the worship of the Great Spirit. Obeisance is made to mammon, not to God, by the overwhelming majority. This is responsible for all the troubles, difficulties and conflicts which beset you today.

If I say I was Joseph of Arimathea or John the Baptist, would that add one iota of authority? Suppose I said I was the chief of the Iroquois in 1867 in Manitoba, would that help?

At a later date came the remark, "As you are the mouthpiece, where does this knowledge come from?" It brought the reply:

It comes from the infinite source and streams through countless beings, each charged with particular tasks to ensure that as much of its purity and pristine beauty should be preserved. There is a great host of beings, ranging from what you might call the masters. They are beyond such descriptions. They are those who can be regarded as the supreme generals in the divine army, each with allotted tasks.

They are very highly organised to ensure not only that the truths shall permeate your world, but that the power of the spirit should reach it in ever-increasing measure. The power is the power of life itself. Spirit is life, life is spirit. And whatever is registered is equivalent to the Great Spirit in essence if not in degree. I hope I make myself clear.

What you have to recognise is that all of us work under direction, that we are not lone individuals. I have just returned from what I might call my real spiritual home in spheres where I belong. I have been engaged in counsel with those who sent me. I have heard more about the supreme plan, the parts we have played, where we are advancing, where we are consolidating.

I went to seek counsel with those who sent me to do their bidding, to learn of the progress that has been made and to obtain direction for work that is still to be done.

Always when I return to those inner spheres I am aware of the perfection of the plan that was devised by superior beings who belong to the hierarchy and marvel at the efficiency of its superb organisation. And so I come back with the reinforced assurance that no matter how dark, difficult and troubled your world is, the power of the Great Spirit will prevail.

Like others, I have recharged myself at the fount of all power so that I can continue to serve in the time that lies before me. It is a source of some satisfaction to learn from those who have the direction of these matters that they consider the plan is being fulfilled. It is here to stay in your world. It will not be driven back. It will not be sporadic as it has been in ages gone by. There is nothing that can prevent the power of the spirit in constantly increasing measure making its sublime influence felt in your world.

So there is no cause for pessimism. Let those who fear the morrow and quake in their shoes hide themselves in their corners. Those who are privileged to have glimpses of the greater glory, and realise what is behind us, must remain optimistic as to what the morrow will bring forth.

Explaining to another visitor why he always rejects thanks the guide said:

It is a rule I have made for the simple reason which I have explained many times. I regard it as a privilege to serve. Therefore, if I succeed in helping then I am fulfilling my self-imposed mission. Thus gratitude should be expressed to the Great Spirit who gives us this chance.

I volunteered to come and share whatever I have learned with those who would accept it. If I succeed that is my reward. It is a cause of great rejoicing for me that in a few short years I have been able to spread the knowledge of spiritual realities among so many.

To have been able to do this makes my heart full of rejoicing. I wish I could reach many more, so that they could enjoy the radiance that comes with knowledge. Something I never understand is why they prefer ignorance to knowledge, superstition to truth, and theology to inspiration. This is a human frailty that is past my comprehension.

I know that yours has not been an easy path to tread. Isn't it strangee that all those who have the great knowledge have to earn it through difficulties and that this is part of the pattern? No, it is not strange, it has to be that way.

It is necessary to warn you that I am not the epitome of all wisdom and truth and knowledge. I am only a soul who has lived a few more years than you have and had experiences on higher planes of being. These have enabled me to acquire some of the great truths, simple in essence. Because I have found them illuminating and helpful, I have retraced my steps to offer to share this knowledge with any who are ready to receive it.

But I am a very human being. I am not infallible. I can make mistakes. I am imperfect, though it may seem from the picture that is painted of me in books and periodicals that I have attained the summit of perfection. I am very grateful that these truths have been and are being accepted by a growing number of people who are disillusioned with what has been taught them.

I am always grateful when I find that what I have to say helps others to have a clearer picture of themselves, the world in which they live, the purpose of their being on earth and to tell them what. is beyond the few years you spend on your planet.

I have nothing complicated to say,` no intricate doctrines to teach, but merely an interpretation of the natural laws and how they work. Always my appeal is to reason. I know that an understanding of these laws can come only when you realise it is a reasonable one. It is not to blind faith that our appeal is made.

If there comes from our world any teaching claiming to emanate from higher sources and it causes your reason to revolt and insults your intelligence, then I always say, "Reject it." If we cannot win your co-operation by reason, then we are not worthy of being called guides.

Several times in recent years, Silver Birch has warned against "guide worship." Here he gives his reasons:

No guide is perfect. We can make mistakes; only the Great Spirit never makes any mistakes. We are all human beings and are subject to error. I have always said that whatever is offered from our world must pass the bar of your reason. I have earned your love and affection because I have never said to you anything that I did not believe was true.

I have never ordered, or sought to compel, but have given you what I consider are guide lines (that is a good phrase) which bring you the best spiritual results. Do not confuse material results with spiritual ones. Sometimes what seems to be your worst material disaster can prove to be your greatest spiritual benefit.

You look at every problem from the earthly standpoint; we look at every problem from the spiritual standpoint; often they are not the same. To you, passing to our world is a sorrow. For us passing to our world is a case for rejoicing.

You cannot judge with your finite minds the truth of every situation. As I said before, where knowledge cannot help, have faith in what has been revealed to you. But when all is said and done you have free will. How you live yourr lives is your responsibility and nobody else's. Nor can you live the lives of others no matter how close they may be.

What they do is their responsibility and not yours. Were this not the case then divine judgement would be poorer than the earthly scales of justice. You will receive spiritually what you have earned. And you will pay spiritually for what you have failed to earn. That is the law and it is perfect in its operation. It is our function to remind you that of ourselves we are nothing. We are all emissaries of the Great Spirit. If we succeed in making the divine will and the divine power accessible to others, then we should be thankful for the opportunities and rejoice that we are succeeding in the tasks assigned to us.

Because of the attention that has been given to the simple truths I am able to enunciate, with the help of those in my world who use me as their instrument, just as I use my medium, there does sometimes emerge a picture which hardly bears any reality to myself.

I was asked, and agreed, to retrace my footsteps to share what I have discovered with those who are ready to receive it. I make no claim to being infallible. I have not come to the end of my progress. But whatever it is that I have discovered and learned, I offer it freely if it is helpful to those prepared to receive it.

It is a source of some satisfaction to find that through the years the teachings, which are not mine, help those in sorrow, trouble and difficulty. These have shown there is a path all can tread and that, when followed, it brings them an understanding of themselves, of the infinite power that is responsible for all life and bestows on every living being a portion of its own divinity, thus providing a link in an unbreakable chain.

Those who qualify as guides know it is wrong for them to be worshipped. Worship should be accorded to the Great Spirit, the perfect epitome of love, wisdom, truth, knowledge, revelation and understanding. We must not allow any deviation from the direction where all thanks should be given, where worship should occur and where there should be an attempt to greater attunement between the Great Spirit and His children. Your love is always welcome. It is only because I find love in your world that makes it possible for me to continue my mission. If I succeed in earning love then I am fulfilling the task that was assigned to me. I will continue to take from it the warmth which helps me when I come to your cold world.

To fulfil yourself is the most important of all achievements. This is one of the objects of our returning to your world, to teach people how to fulfil themselves, to attain self-regeneration. This is the only way in which your world will enjoy all its bounty and enable its inhabitants to live in peace, harmony, co-operation and love instead of the fratricidal strife that exists in far too many places.

Despite the fact that we are comparatively few in number the plan continues to unfold. Progress is constantly being made. Always more and more pilgrims are finding their feet placed on pathways of certainty. And this is all to the good.

Greeting a husband and wife who said they have received

much help and inspiration from the published accounts of his philosophy, the guide said:

It is always good to learn that the teachings of which I am privileged to be only the mouthpiece help those to whom they are addressed. When we first began this mission we were only a small handful. Then with the aid of earthly co-operators these simple but profound truths of the spirit were printed. How fortunate it is that in an ever-increasing number of minds they found a lodgement.

When I was asked to relinquish what I had attained because it was felt I could be of service to your world, I agreed to come, though I was told the task would be far from easy.

It is very, very difficult to leave spheres of radiance and brilliance where you enjoy the company of evolved beings to work in your dark, dank, unattractive physical world. But fortunately we have been able to make friends in many lands. Now through this co-operative effort we can find warmth in hearts and minds here and elsewhere, so that working close to earth has its brief moments of consolation.

When you tell me, as others have said, that I have helped them, then it brings a little more warmth into the coldness which surrounds all those who have to penetrate your earthly conditions.

After he has spoken to visitors, Silver Birch always says a few words to circle members. One of them inquired: "How are you? Nobody ever seems to ask you that question."

I am fortunate in that I do not have to suffer from the problems or ailments of your world. I enjoy radiant health. I do not get older as you measure age.

I was not referring to that.

I hope I will continue to grow in spiritual maturity. Don't you have any problems?

Only when we come back to your world.

I did not think the spirit world was such a bed of roses, as we are supposed to be exactly as we were on leaving here.
I suppose it depends where you are in the spirit world. Even roses have thorns.

Don't you ever get problems?
Yes, but only with the mission on which I am engaged. That is why I withdraw from your world to take counsel with those who sent me, to receive their direction, to hand in my report and to be told what, if anything, should be done when I return to your world again. We have problems, but they are concerned with the unfolding of the divine plan.

The guide asked two circle members who are breaking fresh ground by spreading spirit truths in their locality, "Do you have problems?"

"Only relative ones, he was told. "We are grateful for any service we can give."
You are very privileged. It is always my wish that you will one day be enabled to see what is spiritually around and about you. Thus you would have an ever greater realisation of the work on which you are engaged.

Answering a question from another, member the guide said:
We are still in command of the ship. We do everything that lies in our power. But we are subject to the limitations of earth, to the conditions it provides. We cannot always do what we would like. We have to work with subtle forces that are very delicate. Unless they are completely controlled there is little we can do.

When there is complete control, and the conditions are right in your world and in your surroundings, then we can move matter and make it respond to our will. But it is not always possible. So we have to do the best we can under prevailing circumstances. But about the end result we are positive.

People can delay, hinder and obstruct, but they cannot prevent the divine plan from fulfilling itself in your world. People are the greatest obstacles to their own progress. Stupidity, ignorance, superstition, greed, the lust for power, these rule and prevent your world from being the kingdom of heaven that it could be.

There is plenty for all materially, and there is more than enough spiritually. So we must press on, seeking for means to help those who are ready to be helped. It is the process of getting ready that is the difficulty. We must wait until they experience the catalyst that makes them look within, because if they look without there is no help coming.

Because of what has been achieved in the lives of those associated with the work in which we are all engaged, we are certain that all will be well, however temporary difficulties may seem to provide obstacles. There is such a tremendous power available for all of you. If you are passive, quiescent, receptive, attuned and co-operative, it can fill and flood your being and make you the means of helping not only humans but also the animals.

Many of you promised to come back and do this work. While you are on earth do all you can to fulfil yourselves. When all is said and done, you will finally assess yourselves, not on the gold, silver, jewellery or property that you acquired. You will judge yourself by your spiritual passport. This will declare unerringly who and what you are spiritually.

Asked, "When a medium passes on, does the guide find another human instrument through whom to work?" Silver Birch responded:

It depends on the work that has to be done. In the old days when there were what you describe as physical phenomena, there were in charge guides who had mastered the difficult techniques involved. Some of them, when their instrument passed on, continued to work with other physical mediums.

This is very rarely the case with mental mediums because it involves a much closer co-operation between the guide and the instrument. It is not only a question of blending their auras, but in some cases even helping to become part of their larger selves.

This is such an intimate relationship that, when the instrument passes, the guide's work is done. Usually he returns to that sphere where he belongs. Thus, when in time my instrument joins me, I will not communicate, or try to do so, through another one. I have spent too many years training my instrument to wish to start all over again elsewhere.

In my case the association began from birth. Though the work entailed was of such a character that it had to be done without the instrument's awareness, it meant that we had to keep on building the necessary spiritual and' etheric links to ensure that communication becomes as easy as possible.

When awareness and realisation dawn, and the instrument begins to start development, there comes the other difficult task of learning how to control the subconscious mind so as to be able to use such organs as are necessary to make all communication easy.

Asked about his age, the guide replied: I am as old as the wisdom I try to teach.

I have been privileged to observe some of the wonders due to the workings of those natural laws to which I refer. I have seen how they manifest in worlds which you have yet to tread. Because of what I have seen and learned to prize, I have retraced my footsteps in the hope that some will share this knowledge that will help them to live as they should, with the spirit predominating and matter responding to its divine guidance.

Chapter Two

DOES FREE WILL EXIST?

THE question of free will is one that has dogged man through the centuries. Can we change the course of our lives? Do we have absolute or partial free will?

Silver Birch always welcomes difficult cult questions. Since some regard free will as a thorny problem, it is apposite to devote a chapter to it. Answering a visitor, the guide said:

It is part of the complementary aspect of the law that man and woman help to make the whole. Intuition can help where reason cannot give the answer. You are being given an opportunity to fulfil yourselves. You have free will. You may make your choice.

Life is not chance, accident or even coincidence. The whole of life is governed by immutable natural law. Whatever aspect of being you examine, it is due to natural law. Human beings are not outside the operation of natural law. They are integral parts of it.

The law has operated at a time when you have a choice to make. It is for you to make that choice. You have been led by those who love you. It is love that directs your footsteps. And that love is capable of guiding you if you will allow it to do so.

Love, like life, is indestructible. The things of matter must perish because by their very nature they are ephemeral. The things of the spirit are eternal. Love is a quality of the spirit. Love endures, love survives, love, as your Bible says, is the fulfilling of the law.

"Do all the paths lead to the same place, or do they lead nowhere?" the guide was asked.

The word "place" is difficult. If I might put it my way, all paths lead to the one great divine source of creation. The Great Spirit, what you call "God," is infinite. So there must be an infinite number of paths leading to the Great Spirit, the epitome of perfect love and wisdom.

The Great Spirit is life, and life is spirit. All that is endowed with life has the quality of divinity as part of its heritage of birth. And all the beings who inhabit your planet are engaged on an eternal pilgrimage, pursuing paths that must lead in the ultimate to the one divine goal.

It does not matter what the path is as long as the pilgrim treads it with honesty of purpose, sincerely seeking to fulfil himself, acquit himself and express those gifts with which he has been endowed so that others can be enriched for his presence on earth.

Many young people today are wondering if this planet will survive for very long because of what man is doing to it.

The planet will survive.

Will man?

Yes, man will survive too. There is a limitation placed by natural law on what man can do to the planet on which he lives. He cannot destroy the whole of the planet and all that it contains. Now this is part of man's free will, his choice as to whether he will rise to the divinity within him or whether he will fail. In that case he will not fulfil himself. He will pass to our world unequipped and unready and have to learn all over again.

No man, and no combination of men, have the power to thwart divine will. They can delay, they can harass and they can impede. Infinite wisdom and love rule the universe. These will prevail because that is the law.

Here the visitor said: "We have destroyed many things which can never return to what they were. This applies to much of what was in the ground and it is a limited place that we inhabit."

But it has tremendous potentialities. There is much to be revealed in your world, much to be discovered. You are not at the end of evolution: You are still in its early stages.

Those who are familiar with the truths of the spirit never despair. Their optimism is based on the knowledge that has been revealed to them. With that knowledge they can have complete faith in the overriding power.

In its long history your world has had many disasters. Man has survived them. Man has progressed in spite of himself. He will continue to evolve because evolution is part of the natural law. And spiritual evolution is part of that same law.

At another circle meeting came the question, "How far is free will dependent on karma, for example?" The reply was:

The whole of life is regulated by natural laws. Nothing is left to freakishness, to miracles or to chance. All is cause and effect, sowing and reaping, otherwise the universe would be chaotic. You have evidence of the infinite plan of an infinite intelligence in the operation of natural laws wherever you look.

It is to be seen in the sequence of the seasons, the movement of planets and galaxies, the ebb and flow of tides, the growth of a myriad forms of floral life, where natural law reigns supreme. So there is the limit which the divine power has placed because nothing can occur beyond the framework of natural law. But there are laws within laws. There are not only physical laws, there are mental and spiritual ones.

You live, you breathe, you exist, you have your being because from the moment of conception spirit begins to associate with matter in individuated form and gradually that individuality unfolds.

It is part of the plan that you should have an element of free will, the power and the ability to make choices in certain circumstances. Used for its best and highest, you can play your part in the spiritual unfoldment and evolution of the race, the world, the universe and the cosmos because your spirit is part of the Great Spirit.

You share in the divinity that is responsible for all that exists everywhere. You are the Great Spirit in microcosm. All that the Great Spirit has of that infinity you have and you will have eternity in which to unfold it.

You can wake up tomorrow morning at an hour later or earlier, or you can stay in bed if you like. You can go for a walk or drive a car. You can lose your temper and hope to find it again. There is a variety of things you can do for which you have the free will.

But you cannot stop the sun from shining, you cannot halt the tempest; these are beyond your power. Your free will is limited because your choice is restricted. There is another limitation placed on your free will. It is the mental and spiritual stage which you have reached in your development. You are free to kill, but your character will ensure that you refrain. So even when you have choices these are limited by who and what you are at the time. Like many things in the universe you have a paradox. You have free will within limitations all the time.

Now I must go a stage further because you introduced the question of karma. This too is a very important consideration because many of those who have work to do in your world chose to do it beforehand. Though awareness may not come immediately, the choice imposes another restriction in free will.

Our consciences, are they really ours or those of the guides because they are connected with free will?

You are receiving and transmitting stations. It is very seldom that you construct your own thoughts. Your radio and television have channels, vibrations-frequencies is the right word-to which they can be attuned. So you have your frequency. That enables you to receive thoughts, ideas, suggestions, inspiration, guidance and a variety of ideas from those on your wavelengths. As you receive them they are tinctured with your individuality and sent on their way so that others capture them.

All this is determined by your evolution. The higher spiritually you are evolved the greater is the thought that can reach you. And, because of that, the greater will its effect be as you transmit it and send it on its way.

When the subject was raised again, the guide replied:

Nobody has perfect free will. It is free will within a restricted range. Your will is subject to circumstances which you cannot control. The soul knows before it reincarnates what it has to achieve. It may take a long time for awareness to dawn.

The soul has the awareness imprinted within it. If that awareness does not dawn, then it will have to reincarnate again. If the awareness does come, then it will begin to fulfil the purpose of its incarnation.

I cannot change human nature. It is very malleable material. It can respond to the highest and pitifully can fall to the lowest. This is the great purpose of earthly incarnation. You have within you all the divine possibilities. You have a physical body that comes from the earth, but its animation is derived from this vitalising spirit.

You have the choice as to how you order your existence, as to whether you give priority to spirit or to matter. That is the nature of the human problem. But you must help those who come to you wherever you can. When you cannot, leave them. For all who are brought to you it is their opportunity to find themselves. If they succeed, express gratitude for your chance to serve. But if they fail, feel sorry for them.

When another visitor asked about free will, Silver Birch took the opportunity to explain about its relationship to time.

The question was direct. "How does free will operate?" The woman guest explained her interest "arose from something I read in Two Worlds where you refer to time as being the eternal present." She added:

"If I look back through my life I can see all the intersections, decisions I made, the operation of cause and effect, the whole chain. Supposing I had the gift -of looking into the future. I should see what is lined up for me. But if that is the case, where does my free will come in?" The guide replied:

Forgive me for saying this, but you are a little confused. Time is the eternal present. It is not past or future. It is your relationship to time that determines your past and future. If you visualise time-this is very hard to conveyas a circle which is constantly moving round, the point where you touch it is what you call your present. The part where you have touched it is what you call your past. The part you have yet to touch is what you call your future. But so far as time is concerned it has no past or future.

What you call "looking into the future" is only that ability through clairvoyance or attunement when you. escape the three-dimensional boundaries of the physical world and see what will be your future. You behold the effect of the cause you put into motion, what your free will has created. But this does not affect time itself, only your relation to it.

Chapter Three

REINCARNATION—A SPIRIT VIEW

OF all the imponderables affecting life here and hereafter, reincarnation probably heads the list. It is noteworthy that for many years Silver Birch's views on this highly controversial problem were in direct contrast to those of his medium.

Karma, it is said, also plays its part in rebirth. Believers maintain it is the only logical explanation as to why some are born beggars and others kings; why some have appalling mental and physical handicaps when others do not.

Those who do not share this outlook say it offers a ready-made excuse for life's misfortunes and unfortunates.

Here are Silver Birch's views. Asked "Why is there such a divided opinion among guides and Spiritualists on reincarnation?" he answered:

Because some know and some don't. It is a question of experience. It takes a long time, as you count it, for this fact to be appreciated. People can be in our world for what you call ages and still be unaware of this truth. You must realise that the world of spirit is graded. It is not a one plane surface, so to speak, where all are of an equal level of attainment.

It is graded in spiritual development. You will find that the higher the ascent in this spiritual scale, the more recognition is there of the fact that there is reincarnation, because it happens, but not in the facile form that is so often propounded.

Asked if reincarnation was voluntary or because some purpose had to be achieved, the guide replied, "Both."

So I take it that because we see the purpose we wish to be reborn.

Yes, I could not put it more succinctly.

Therefore, in effect, it is compulsion?

It depends how you define compulsion. Nobody orders you to do it. But if you feel you are compelled to do it then you could call it compulsion. Nobody will order you to reincarnate in your world. But you will feel you have a lesson to learn, a service to perform, a wrong to redress, a kindness to be done that you had failed before and will want to do it because you know it is best for you to do so.

We are told we live for ever with our closest loved ones after leaving the earth plane. Can you explain what happens when our loved one reincarnates?

This is not the problem that it seems because it is an attempt to equate a spiritual happening by a physical measurement. You have heard me say many times that the personality expressed on earth is only a fragment of the total individuality. I have compared it to facets of a large diamond.

Facets can incarnate and others can reincarnate. There can be temporary earthly incursions when this happens and there is separation between the facets of the diamond. But where the law of affinity is at work there will be no such separation.

"Is not the teaching of reincarnation a confusion arising from the subjective heavens of `the happy hunting grounds' originally given to teach the reality of the earthly life to those who died in infancy?" asked a reader.

If the questioner likes to think so, he or she is entitled to do so, but that will not alter its truth. Facts are facts, whether you like them or not, or whether you agree with them or not. The wise individual is the one who tries to understand when confronted with a fact or its implications. But if it does not make sense to you, then reject it. If it appears to you foolish, reject it. As you grow, your capacity to understand will increase and you will find what you may have rejected before now makes sense.

A circle member, referring to another reader's question on the population explosion, asked: "Where do all these souls come from? If there is a certain number of souls to come back to earth, there must be a reservoir. We are told not to produce too many children. But if mankind goes on producing them they would be born. Consequently where do these souls come from?"

It may be the wrong word to use, but your question is based on a misconception. You do not create souls in your world. What you do is to create the channels for souls to manifest. Spirit, the primal essence, is, infinite, and infinity cannot be measured. What you do is to provide a means whereby spirit can incarnate and become individuated.

You, as spirit, have always existed. As individual spirit you started from the moment of conception. There are others who existed in your world before and who have a task to perform, redress to make, or something to achieve. They wait until they find the right vessels who will provide them with the opportunities for what they have to do.

I thought that all human souls gradually evolved from every stage of life.

No, that is the physical ancestry. Spirit has always existed.

What is the essential difference between old and new souls? Where does the new spirit come from? Who decides into what conditions they incarnate or reincarnate? The guide answered:

The essential difference between an old and a new soul is one of age. Obviously the old is older than the new. "Where does a new soul come from?" This question is very loosely phrased. Souls do not come from anywhere. Spirit has always been in existence. Spirit will always be in existence. It is the primal essence, the life force, the divine. It says in your Bible that "God is spirit."

If the questioner means, "Where does the individual soul come from?" then I say that at the moment of conception a particle of spirit incarnates to begin to express individuality on earth.

A circle member asked, "Is that then a part of the totality of the Great Spirit?"

Yes, that is why you are linked for ever with the Great Spirit. You cannot be cut off, you cannot be banished, you cannot be excommunicated. You are for all time bound up inextricably with the power which is life, no matter what manifestation it takes.

Another member asked, "But does the individual life start before that moment?"

You are using words which make it difficult. Do you mean, "Has the individuality yvhich is expressed from the moment of conception existed before?" Yes, sometimes, but not in the same personality which. is now beginning to be expressed on earth. As spirit is infinite, it will take a long time to comprehend infinity.

The next question was, "Is there an organisation in the spirit world to control reincarnation, to prevent mistakes being made?"

All these matters are simply resolved by the operation of natural law. You decide if you should incarnate. You do so at a time when you have a greater awareness and realise what can be achieved by becoming embodied in the earthly world. It does not require any group or organisation of beings. This is a matter the soul decides for itself.

Is each incarnation progressive, or is it possible to end further down the ladder than when one started? Replied the guide:

All life, especially that of the spirit, is progressive. I am referring specifically to the spiritual because it is the one that really matters. Once you have knowledge, wherever it was gained, then as you apply it automatically you grow spiritually and advance. And advance is always progression, though it will take eternity to achieve perfection.

In discussions on reincarnation sceptics ask how blue babies and the mentally deficient can possibly learn any lesson from earth life. Many Spiritualists take this difficult question on trust, knowing we will understand one day. But if we cannot answer the sceptic he may remain one. Can you suggest the best way to answer without getting involved in abstruse discussion?

There is no answer to the sceptic. The sceptic must find out for himself until he is satisfied. Then the scepticism will vanish. We are not theologians. This is not a matter of argument or a discussion in which you score points. This is a spiritual process in which awareness has to come to individuals.

As they achieve awareness they will understand some of the mysteries of life. They will not understand them all because if you could do so you would not be on earth. Earth is your school where you learn your lessons. Gradually, as you learn them, and knowledge comes, so your awareness grows. With it comes your ability to receive and understand more.

That is what the whole purpose of life is about. It is not for me to argue, to be challenged to debate. I can only enunciate certain fundamental truths which have endured – and will endure. If they cannot be accepted, I am sorry. There is nothing I can do about it.

You say the soul is divided into many parts. Only one part can come to earth. The others are progressing in other spheres. Can you amplify this?

We have to use words which are very poor symbols for that which is beyond all your language. Words are phy~ical. The soul is non-physical. How do we interpret the non-physical in physical language? This is a great problem of what you call semantics. To me the soul is that portion of the divinity within each one of you, what you call God, and I the Great Spirit. There are no means of measuring souls in terms that you can understand. The soul is the life force, the dynamic, the vitality, the real essence, the divinity.

You think of souls in terms of personalities and individuals. If I ask, who are you? I don't know how you would answer. Giving me your name does not tell me who you are. That is only the name by which you are called. Who are you, the individual, the judge, the thinker, the one who expresses love and is capable of manifesting all the emotions that form the spectrum of human experience in your world? That is the soul.

You live on earth because the, soul provides animation for the physical body. When the soul withdraws, the physical body, having no animation,.dies. That soul has not a name, such as you are called by in your world. Because it is divine it is infinite. And being infinite it is capable of an infinite number of manifestations. That soul has many aspects. I use the simile of a diamond with many facets.

Those facets can incarnate into your world at differing times to gain experience, to help the other facets in the diamond's evolution towards perfection.

Where you have affinities, which is rare, it is because they are two facets of the one diamond incarnating at the same time on earth. That is why there is a complete harmony between them. They are parts of the one whole. This brings us to the subject of reincarnation. Here you have facets of the diamond incarnating into your world to add knowledge, development and experience that will help the diamond in its evolution.

Can you explain more fully the "group soul" which you describe as a diamond with many facets? Are they family groups, people in the same state of spiritual development, those with the same interests, or what else?

If the questioner uses the word "family" in its literal sense, as you understand it, being confined to people who have blood ties or relationships due to marriage, then this does not apply to group souls. Earthly ties, which are purely material, do not necessarily continue when the body has served its purpose.

In spiritual relationships, you have in the supreme case affinities or in the lesser instances kinship. Physical relationships are conditions not based on eternal principles, the only ones that will endure. Group souls, when referring to their human aspects, are composed of individuals who have a spiritual kinship. Automatically they are drawn to one another because they are the facets of the one diamond. It can be, and it does happen, that for purposes of work to be done fragments of the diamond incarnate into your world to have the kind of experience which will help the larger self.

Are we all not parts of the same soul?

That is very difficult. This is the old trouble when you have to define the words you use. We are all part of the same spirit because spirit is the substance of life. Soul, for the purpose of strict definition, is individuated spirit. So in those terms, all life is one, all spirit is one, but spirit being infinite has an infinite variety of manifestations.

Spiritually we are all one, but our souls are individual. In your world people group together. They combine for specific labour or service. In our world there are groupings to achieve functions which are part of the plan. Some of these groupings are not so intact-it is very hard to find words for spiritual conditions-as others. Speaking generally, . when there are group souls there is a kinship or affinity between those individual souls in your world.

Would it be true to say that this in a way is the first step towards a further development which will come when all souls become one?

No, all souls do not become one.

There is, at the moment, a group soul composed of individuals. Cannot one picture, in millions of years, this process developing until all mankind becomes one, the complete group soul?

No, because the process is eternal, it can have no ending. Perfection is never attained. Each step towards it reveals another which must be ascended. It says in your Bible that he who loseth himself findeth himself. This is an attempt to explain the great mystery of individuality, that. you become, as you progress, more of an individual but less of a person. That is a complication, isn't it?

Personality is the expression of earthly characteristics that enable recognition to be achieved between one and another. Individuality is an expression of the soul where its qualities are developed. As this process is being achieved so you are less of a person, as you understand it physically, but more of an individual spiritually.

Would it be right to say that only God is perfect and that naturally we cannot achieve perfection?

You cannot become perfect because if you did it would be the end of evolution. And evolution in essence must be a continuing process. There is no limit to development. Divinity does not have a vanishing point; it is infinite.

It is a very hard conception to grasp, but it is like learning. You cannot say you come to the end of learning, or to the acquisition of wisdom or understanding. You cannot put a period to compassion. You cannot say that you have reached the finality of love. These are divine qualities which are capable of infinite development as the soul reaches out, more and more, towards its goal, which is the attainment of perfection.

We still then have a lot of work in store for us.

You will be busy for a long time. You need not fear being spiritually unemployed or being made spiritually redundant.

At another circle the guide was asked, "What is meant by twin souls?" It brought the response

Twin souls are when the affinities, which are the two halves of the perfect whole, come together. There are affinities for every soul in the universe, but they do not often meet in the same incarnation.

Where there are souls, complementary to one another, who have earned the right to meet the other half of its being in one incarnation, there you truly achieve heaven on earth. Twin souls are what the words entail, a likeness between two similars. They are at the same stage of growth and evolution and thus will go forward together. You have heard me say occasionally to people, "You are, affinities.

A circle member commented, "I presume twin souls could meet for a few years and one lose the other."

Only physically, but at least for the time they are together they are experiencing all the radiance that comes when unity is achieved on all planes of being.

The same member, thinking aloud, said, "If they have knowledge then the radiance would be even greater." Another member put his question: "If there are twin souls who have reached the same stage of evolution, what is the purpose for some being apart in this present incarnation? One would have thought automatically they would have earned the right to be together."

You mean they have come together and parted physically. That can only be temporary. If they are affinities the whole urging of their souls will bring them together with the strongest pull that is possible. Just like the lodestar, the magnetic attraction will draw them together because, although two, spiritually they are one.

It could be part of a twin soul's development for them to be apart in one incarnation.

These are minor difficulties that you raise. Whether they are apart and still a part of one another, the essential factor is that if they are two halves of the one soul, all other physical differences and happenings cannot affect the fundamental process that brings them together. Don't confuse physical happenings with spiritual realities. What is of the spirit must endure.

The next question was, "Why are some beings never incarnated into matter and others are?"

There is part of the hierarchy that has never incarnated into matter because it has a purpose to serve in helping the governance of the universe. There are celestial beings who have never taken earthly form. It is not necessary for them to endure earth expression to attain a growth essential for their larger life. They are inherently part of the higher reaches of the spiritual realms. Some of these are what you call masters or the shining ones. There are these beings in existence.

Can a heavy karmic debt be cancelled when, during earth life, there is a complete spiritual change which reorientates one to love and service? Or does it still have to be paid?

Natural law is always cause and effect. The operation of natural law cannot be cancelled. Natural law is almost mechanical in that effect must follow cause, as effect contains within itself what will be the succeeding cause, and thus the chain is endless.

No cancellation can take place. If an individual, to use the words of the question, reorientates himself or herself and begins to serve, then automatically this discharges a debt. The amount of the service that is rendered will in time reduce the debt until it is out of existence. That is when the balance has been achieved.

Is it karma that thousands are killed in wars, accidents, by disease and starvation? Can a soul die before its time? Are wars inevitable? If so, is this part of a nation's karma?

The questioner is wrong in saying it is the soul that dies. The soul cannot die. Karma is only a word that means the operation of natural law. Sowing and reaping are part of the law of cause and effect. No one can evade the operation of natural law.

This is the means devised by the Great Spirit to ensure that ultimately divine justice must be forthcoming. If it were possible to abrogate this natural law and to interfere with the sequence of cause and effect, it would make a mockery of divine justice. The natural law ensures that each receives spiritually exactly that to which he is entitled, no more and no less. This law applies not only to individuals but to nations, which after all are assemblies of individuals.

It is part of the law that the period of incarnation is determined by the soul. But it is possible, because of man's free will and sometimes for other factors to arise that this determining period can be changed.

As to whether wars are inevitable, this is a question that human beings in your world must resolve for themselves. They cannot have all the benefits of free will without some of the disadvantages. If beings in your world choose to exercise their free will and their choice is to wage war, that is the measure of their responsibility.

This led a member to comment: "You said a soul decides the period of its incarnation. Would this apply to all souls, such as undeveloped ones? Would they have the judgement, knowledge and wisdom? Are all souls equal in these matters?"

There is a difference between the amount of wisdom a soul can express when it incarnates into an earthly body as compared with that it possesses before incarnating. The amount of wisdom that can be expressed in your world is very limited because all spiritual expression is restricted by the faculties of the physical body. Before incarnation the soul knows, in the vast majority of cases, what path it is to tread.

If the soul knows the experiences and sufferings that lie ahead, then does it not know the results of its life?

When the guide answered, "Yes," he was asked, "If that is so, what is the point if it knows beforehand what it has to undergo and the result?"

So that the soul can gain the necessary experiences to qualify for the work it has to do when it comes to our world. The fact that it knows beforehand does not mean that it has achieved the soul growth which is necessary for its evolution.

You can read all the books in your world, but that knowledge must be reinforced by experience. It is experience and your reaction to it which determines the growth which you will achieve. This is the whole purpose of your earthly incarnation.

A young journalist asked a question about air disasters. "I am puzzled because I cannot decide whether these events are planned because the victims and their relatives are repaying some karmic debt. If they are planned, why do people have premonitions of them? These premonitions sometimes appear to change the whole course of events."

This is quite a question. I don't like the word "planned." It presupposes that there is a deliberate attempt to plan a tragedy in your world. Everything that happens is due to cause and effect. As to the victims-I must use your language-of these tragedies, do not forget there is another side to the picture.

Death to people in your world is to be feared. But death to us is something of the nature of rejoicing. There are many in our world who cry when babies are born into yours. We rejoice when death brings freedom to those who die.

It may be hard to understand, but destiny has its part in the great eternal scheme. This is a complex subject in which fate and free will play their parts. Both are true. There is a restricted free will within the destined fate. This is the simplest way that I can put it. As to premonitions, these occur because individuals momentarily remove themselves from their usual threedimensional perceptions and are able to experience, however fleetingly, time as it exists in its own sphere. What you must try to realise is that time is an eternal present. It is your earthly relationship to time that determines what you call past and future. Time itself has no past and no future. If you escape the three-dimensional barriers and get in tune with time as it really is, then you are aware of what is the future to you at the present time.

Now as to what use is made of .this awareness is another matter. It can appeal purely on a super-physical level or on a spiritual one. The purely psychic is not the same as the spiritual. You have what you call "extra-sensory perception" which can have no relationship to your spiritual nature, but be merely an extension of your physical senses.

After listening to comments from circle members Silver Birch said:

Life is a polarity. Life is full of an infinite number of experiences. Without peril there is no safety, without darkness there is no light, without storm there is no sunshine. Life is not a monotone; it is a contrast. It is only in the contrast that you appreciate what it is all about. You must have the polarity. You must have action and reaction. They may be opposite but they are also equal.

When the words "calamity" and "tragedy were used in the ensuing conversation among members, Silver Birch said:

I never teach you to look only at the physical aspect. Always try to appreciate that you cannot measure infinity with a physical yardstick. Your world is full of injustices if seen only through physical eyes. But there is compensation as there is retribution. The spiritual ledger is always balanced. Earth is only an infinitesimal part of an eternal life.

Your tragedies are often our boons. Your benefits are often our tragedies. You attach large importance to things which we in our world regard as either trivial or having no spiritual value. I refer to the desire for possessions, for earthly riches, for power for self, for domination. Greed and avarice motivate so many minds in your world.

Of spiritual progress the guide told the reporter:

In the things of the spirit it cannot be easy. If it were then they would not be worth achieving. Spiritual progress is the hardest of all to attain. Every step of the way has to be earned by discipline, endeavour, dedication, selflessness and fidelity. It was never meant to be easy. The prizes of the spirit have to be fought for before they can be won.

If they were easily attained their value would be very little. It is because they are difficult that they are worth while. It is an endless path you are treading. There is no finality in spiritual progress. It is in a way a kind of receding horizon. The nearer you get the more it recedes.

Similarly the more you learn, the more you learn there is to be learned. Progress, like knowledge, truth and wisdom, is infinite. No period can be put to progress. If you have made one step, two, three, or even four, that is an achievement. Each step means more understanding of life's purpose, its reality, the eternal principles on which it is founded, a greater perception of those eternal verities and with that comes a closer attunement.

Attainment leads to attunement. As you achieve a closer harmony with the overriding power of the universe, you become more at one with it. Your life is enriched. You are able to have a real sense of values. The perception is right. The priorities fall into their allotted places. You know what it is that matters and that too often the goals which others want, because they prize them so highly, are not the ones that matter.

When all the riches of earth have gone, the treasures of the spirit will remain untarnished, undiminished, always with that pristine beauty which is theirs.

I am not so concerned with the material progress, which has its place. It is never part of our teaching to ignore the necessities of your physical selves. Unless the body receives what is essential to its rightful growth, the spirit cannot function adequately through it. What has to be accomplished is the harmony between body, mind and spirit so that these three parts of a whole work in unity, all the time ensuring health, well-being, serenity, confidence, resolution and peace.

To seek to develop the spirit and ignore the physical body is just as wrong as to seek to develop the physical body and to ignore the spirit. And it is equally as wrong, to develop the mind and to ignore the other essentials.

Though astrology is not part of Spiritualist philosophy, it is still interesting to read the guide's views on this subject. Asked, "Is there any truth in astrology; can the moment of birth influence one's life?" Silver Birch said:

There is truth in the fact that the whole of life, because it is life, is in a constant state of radiation. Life cannot be inert; life must manifest. To manifest it must do so on a wavelength, or a radiation, or a frequency, which I think is the term today.

Everything in the universe acts and reacts upon everything else and everybody. There are radiations from storms which affect the body. There is a radiation from the sun as its rays give light, strength and growth. There are radiations from trees which having stored energy can release it.

The whole of nature is in a constant state of radiation. You receive radiations from planets. These affect the physical body because they are physical radiations. But there is no radiation or force emanating from any planet that directly affects the spirit. It does so only to the extent that it affects the physical body, which in turn affects the spirit.

A circle member, seeking further clarification, said, "I think the questioner is asking if all people, say for example born on February 1, have similar qualities because of it."

No, that cannot be so because the spirit is superior to matter. Whatever matter is subjected to is never so strong that the incarnating spirit cannot, given the right conditions, triumph over it. In any case, looked at purely physically, every child has inherited certain material characteristics as part of the evolutionary process. These cannot be set aside because of the time that the child was conceived or born.

In addition to all the factors of heredity and environment every incarnating individual is of necessity spirit, whichhas infinite potentiality. It is the spirit that can, if allowed, rule matter and not, unfortunately as is the case with millions, allow matter to predominate over the spirit.

Another questioner asked: "As far as the future is concerned, how far is it fixed? How far is it subject to our own conduct and spiritual outlook? For example, I have had the stars read for me in two cases. Both are rather poor for the next months. This could have a subjective influence on my life if I don't oppose it. One does wonder how to form one's destiny in these circumstances."

The guide quoted from Shakespeare, "The fault, dear Brutus, is not in our stars, but in ourselves that we are underlings." This was followed by his quoting from. Henley's poem: "It matters not how strait the gate. How charged with punishment the scroll. I am the master of my fate; I am the captain of my soul." Then he added:

The planets are physical. They have a radiation, they emit a vibration. You are physical and spiritual. You have within yourself the means of overcoming all the challenges that earthly life offers.

The future is the child of the past. It is the condition you create by your actions and by your thoughts. I spoke about the natural law. One is cause and effect, sowing and reaping. When you plant the seed of a flower, only that flower will grow, not another one.

Thus your future is determined by your past and your present. It is not a punishment inflicted on you from outside. It is the destiny that you make for yourself. If you allow any fear of what the future may bring to enter your consciousness you are helping it to materialise.

Chapter Four

FROM BIRTH TO BEYOND—1

THIS chapter, allied with the next, traces man from birth to what lies beyond. Starting at conception, we examine the problems associated with the physical body, question whether or not the earthly lifespan is predetermined, and consider the guide's views on death and grief.

At what state did man as a spiritual being enter the evolutionary process during the span from amoeba to his present state of development? Was he already in the first living cell?

If the questioner means the human species, then it was not present in the amoeba. But wherever there has been any form of life there has been spirit, because spirit is life and life is spirit. It is true to say there has always been spirit manifesting through every process and form of growth, from the lowest to the highest, from the simple to the most complex.

The human element arises in the gradual development of the amoeba. As part of the evolutionary process there is a constant unfoldment towards the human being. Man becomes man at that time in evolution when man was aware of being man, that is, when man had self-awareness, consciousness. But evolution has always been in existence. Evolution did not have a beginning. It is beginning and endless because it is part of the progress towards perfection.

Could you tell us when the spirit takes up residence in the physical body? Is it at the moment of conception, or the quickening, or when?

I have been asked this many times. I always give the same answer. When there is conception there is life. And where there is life there is spirit.

Would you say that at the actual moment of conception, spirit takes up residence and then grows to a personality?

This is a little more difficult when you introduce words like personality. Life is spirit and spirit is life. They are one and the same. What you call conception means that there is life. If there is no conception there is no life. Therefore spirit' incarnates into matter at the moment of conception.

As to the question of its development, this is more difficult because it depends on a variety of circumstances. The spirit that incarnates at the moment of birth has always existed as spirit. So the question of personality means to what extent is it an aspect or an expression of an individuality, which is something much larger than a personality.

At what point does a fertilised seed become a human being? At what stage precisely in the prenatal existence of a child does it become a human being? Would you say a foetus is a human being?

Yes, from the moment of conception there is life and there is spirit. If there is what you call in your world a miscarriage or an abortion, you have not destroyed the life force. You have merely removed its expression from your world to ours.

When would you say that that prenatal form of life in the womb was really a human being as we understand the term?

It is potentially a human being from the moment of conception and has latent within it all the aspects of humanity.

From the moment of fertilisation?

Just as it has from the moment of conception latent within it all its physical characteristics, so it also has all its spiritual characteristics. It could not have the physical characteristics unless the spiritual characteristics were there, because matter is a shadow of the spirit.

Do I understand you to imply that a spirit has no choice whatever over the vehicle it will use on earth?

No, you do not understand me to say it at all. On the contrary, the spirit has every choice. In the majority of cases the spirit chooses to incarnate through a particular vehicle because it has work to do in your world. It can take a very long time for you to wake up to do the work that you said you were going to do.

Of the physical body, Silver Birch said:

The physical body, from the moment it is born, begins to die. Nothing can change that fact. It is not conceived to achieve permanence in your, world. By nature it knows it has only an ephemeral existence. It must follow the cycle. Gradually it achieves the maturity of physical well-being. Then just as gradually every aspect of the body begins to wear out. What should happen is that the physical body drops away, as I have said many times, when it is ripe, as the apple drops from the tree.

We in our world are not perfect. We have not attained the end of our spiritual progress. We have a long, long way to go. But we utilise what power we can attract when we are confronted with material conditions which make it very difficult for us to work in your world.

I have always said, and will continue to say, we do not possess all knowledge because it is infinite. You in your world are able to have only a smaller amount of knowledge because you are encumbered with physical limitations that do not apply to us.

To a circle member who was very tired Silver Birch said:

When you lack rest, then the body pays the price. Sometimes the price is exacted that you must take to your beds for a complete rest. We cannot preach personal responsibility and tell you that there are exceptions to the operation of this law. Do not try to do too much. The body is only a machine and it must not be overtaxed beyond its capacity.

Another circle member said: "It is so difficult when you say we must take to our beds when we are tired. We know that, but where other people are concerned that we have to look after because they are so much worse than we are, you have to give yourself " The guide replied:

You cannot change the operation of natural laws. I love you all. If I did not love you I would not be here. There are no attractions for us in your world of matter. It is because we love you that we come and work with you and among you. We have nothing to gain by so doing. Many of us have willingly sacrificed what we have attained to serve as best we can.

We do love you with a heart that is filled with affection for you, but we cannot change the laws. You have machines that you call physical bodies. The finest machines in your world are given rest. They are not made to work as your physical bodies are made to work. If you don't rest them the machines break down.

It is your responsibility because it is your body. The Great Spirit has given you intelligence and reason for you to use these divine powers. Do not blame me because I tell you what I know is the truth about the way the universe works. I cannot be false to that which I know, I can only give you ideals to be achieved, spiritual maxims that are based on truth and which when applied to your lives will bring you the richness which should be your natural heritage.

It is for you to decide what to do. We help you to the best of our ability. There are circumstances sometimes beyond our control when our best is not good enough. We cannot interfere with your free will. We have to stand by at times and watch what you do because your decision is important in your evolution.

Are we forgiven then for breaking the law?

Motive is the important consideration.

Is it not true that sometimes in life, because you love somebody and want to help, you deliberately break the law, but do it with the right intention?

All I can say is the law is the law is the law. It will operate because it must operate. If I could interpose between cause and effect it would be very bad indeed. It would be doing a disservice. The law is perfection. How else could it work?

You have said on occasion you can bring laws to bear that would ease a situation.

Yes, we have helped some of you in the times of your greatest despair. What we cannot do is alter the sequence of cause and effect. Nor is any forgiveness involved. I try to be your guide, to point out to you that your body is a machine. It must have rest. If you overwork it cannot function. When it cannot function you have to take to your bed until the machine is ready to work properly.

What I know is that we are all very privileged because of what has been revealed to us. We have also seen what the power of the spirit can do, the wondrous transformation it can make, how it can point the way, give guidance and show each one the ideals to be attained to fulfil themselves. Those are the important matters.

The physical body is the means by which the spirit expresses itself. If you want to have the fullest expression then the physical body must be fit to do so. If you overwork, it cannot fulfil its proper function. That is why the Great Spirit, with infinite wisdom, ordained sleep, so that it can bring refreshment and restore vitality to the physical body.

Look at the order of the seasons in your world, how in the

autumn nature prepares itself for the sleep of winter, awakens in the spring to achieve the full glory of the summer. So your bodies must have rest, refreshment and recuperation. Learn from nature the lesson it has to teach you. Rest is essential.

Silver Birch pointed the moral by referring to two circle members who had suffered ill-health as a result of overwork.

Even with their knowledge they fall by the wayside. When they do then they must have rest. It is our function to help you to help yourselves, to give obedience, not only to the laws of the spirit and mind, but also to those that control your bodies. When you provide this obedience and there is harmony then you are healthy and well.

To a visitor's comment, "I am afraid I don't listen," Silver Birch said:

That is why the Great Spirit gave you ears. You have in your Spiritualism a set of seven principles. One of them is personal responsibility. That is probably the most important one of all. It enshrines a truth which cannot be gainsaid.

You are personally responsible for what you do, not for what anybody else does. There is nobody and nothing that can absolve you from your responsibility. If you do not pay heed you must pay the price. That is the natural law of cause and effect.

The visitor said: "I know about personal responsibility, but I am afraid I never thought of it for myself I always thought of it or everyone else, but I shall remember."

Please do,' because the natural laws will continue to operate irrespective of what you think about them. They are not indifferent, but they are compelled to work their own way, just the same as we are compelled to work along certain lines.

I have always told my friends here that we can only do things in our way and in our time, not in your way and in your time. We are bound by laws, as you are, to ensure that we do what is essential when it is spiritually right. We can pull strings, we can control matter, we can even find money for you when it is necessary, but only in accordance with the operation of natural law.

I always say that you must do whatever you think is right and whatever your conscience gives the direction. You are in the end your own judges and will be able to assess, when looking back, whether the things you did were always right or sometimes wrong. If the motive is to serve, it cannot be wrong. Motive is the paramount consideration.

Remember always that primarily you are spiritual beings expressing yourselves through physical bodies. You are not bodies with spirits, you are spirits with bodies. Strive always so to order your lives that your spiritual nature will rise to the heights.

The subject of lifespan was discussed by the guide when a visiting medium said, "Life seems to run out so quickly and we want to do so much." Silver Birch told him

You have to learn to become philosophical. You must realise that long before you incarnated into matter, there were others, rugged pioneers, hewing out the path, finding it very difficult and wondering what was going to happen when their earthly life ended. But they removed a few of the boulders and made it easier for you to tread where it was so hard for them. If you move a few more boulders this is your contribution. After you will come others. They will continue to keep on moving the boulders until ultimately there are no more to be removed.

Earth is your schoolhouse of experience. It is not perfect, neither are you. You are imperfect beings in an imperfect world trying to express as much of perfection as you can while you are there. So do your best, no more is expected of you. It is important to help those who cross your path to come into their own, to recognise that they are shaped in the divine image, that they have the divine potential and that this power is capable of bringing a beauty, love and radiance into their lives that makes all worth while.

So thank the Great Spirit for the challenges that come to you. As you answer them you are better spiritually as a result. If you find among your associates some who cannot measure up to the task, if their vision has become obscured, bypass them. Work with those who still have the vision splendid of the great purposes to be fulfilled.

Is our lifespan on earth predetermined, or is it a question of physical strength or some other factor?

It is all part and parcel of the one thing. The physical structure, the body, is that which is necessary for the soul to have the experience which is essential for its growth on earth. The two go together. The termination of the earthly period in most cases is known in advance.

You cannot isolate matter from spirit. The two are inextricably bound together, with matter restricting spirit and spirit animating matter. You cannot divide the aspects of your being into isolated compartments. You are a comprehensive whole, with every facet reacting on other facets. All aspects merge, combine and mingle to make up the totality which is you, the soul.

Arising out of that, if, say, a thousand people were drowned simultaneously, were they all ready to go at that particular time? Was the ordained span for their soul growth the same?

It is the use of words which is difficult. When you say "ordained," by whom and by what? The underlying suggestion is that in some way this is a happening arranged by the Great Spirit. But it does not work that way. The natural laws control every aspect of being throughout the vast panorama of life.

At some stage, no matter what scientists may say in your

world, death is inevitable to the physical body. It serves its purpose by releasing the spirit. Thus physical death is equivalent to physical birth. One is the exit of the spirit and the other is its entrance.

Your world regards death as a tragedy, but it is not a tragedy to us. Death is liberation because it is the spiritual birth of a soul. It is its release from all the problems of your world. It is, in the vast majority of cases, a reward, not a punishment. People must not regard death as something to be avoided at all costs, but to recognise it as an integral part of life, the means by which the soul must come into its own.

Though much is heard about the next world, few seem to give thought to preparing for our future life there. Surely we could begin to educate ourselves with this in view, practising the arts instead of watching television. Have you any suggestions?

It always comes back to the question of realisation. If you are aware that you are a spiritual being with a body, that your world is not your permanent abode, that everything physical is ephemeral ... If you are aware that you, the spiritual you, the indestructible you, the you that is divine, will emerge after death to continue the life of infinite progress ...

Then if you are wise, you will behave in such a fashion that automatically you prepare for what is your future existence beyond death. Your actions will be governed by the stage of spiritual awareness you have reached.

Can you explain the cause of earthquakes and the thousands of people, regardless of their spiritual development, killed in them?

Why do you think death is such a disaster? You rejoice when babies are born into your world, but we often cry. We rejoice when people come into our world, but you cry. Death for the majority is not a tragedy for those who die. There may be a temporary problem while adjustment is made, but death brings liberation. Death is the end of the thraldom that earth imposes on the spirit.

You are bound – and I appreciate your problem – to view all your difficulties with earth-time measurement. But you are infinite. If you live on earth for 60, 70 or 100 years, then 100 over infinity is a very small fraction.

There are no accidents in the operation of natural law. You pass from your world at the time appointed for the - spirit. In many cases this is the time the spirit has chosen for its passing before it incarnated into your world.

Reverting to earthquakes and such disasters, we know people survive death, but they suffer for years maybe before they die. Perhaps they are homeless and never have the opportunity to make another home. Do you think that perhaps we are born .into that part of the world for the sake of these experiences?

You cannot escape all the advantages and disadvantages of living in your world. You must experience its darker as well as its brighter sides. The soul will develop not when you are lotus-eaters. The soul will come into its own in times of difficulty, struggle and crisis. I appreciate you cannot understand this because you are measuring according to your earth-time. But from the viewpoint of infinity your difficulties are better for you than all your benefits.

On other occasions came these words:

You have no idea of the wonders, beauty, richness, glory and the radiance of life in our world. It is impossible to find language to describe it for you. Let me say without fear of contradiction that death is often the jailer who unlocks the door of the cell to bring freedom. Everybody in your world has to die. It is part of the law that you cannot live on earth for ever. So it is inevitable that the physical body, when it has fulfilled its function, should be severed from the spiritual body and the soul which endowed it with animation. It is thus that the transitional period can be accomplished and the soul go marching on as part of its eternal pilgrimage.

The next question asked on behalf of a friend was, "Do you agree it is foolish to keep sad anniversaries as it is a waste of good emotion and therefore unwise and quite useless?" The visitor commented, "It is bad enough to dwell on pain when we cannot help ourselves, but actually to force ourselves to dwell on it for one day a year ..."

What would be considered, according to the questioner, as a sad anniversary?

The anniversary of a death. I have come across people who won't do anything on a death anniversary. I suppose they want to be miserable all over again.

It is a sad anniversary for whom?

For the loser, not for the person who has passed, I agree with you. It is a form of selfishness probably.

This is self-pity. This is sorrow for self, bemoaning its loss. No tears need be shed for those who are released from all suffering in your world. The majority of people who come to our world are better for so doing. There is a minority who, because of selfish earthly lives, are still chained to the world of matter.

But for the vast majority it is a release from prison. It is a new-found freedom in which there are the means of expressing all latent gifts. They are able to live in the sunlight of knowledge instead of the darkness of ignorance.

If because of days that have gone there are anniversaries that are sad, why recall them? What is achieved of value to the soul? Nothing! It is always unwise to look backward. It is better to live one day at a time and to greet every morning with joyous anticipation as a herald of opportunity to grow, expand, unfold and develop spiritually. That is the way of wisdom.

"It is so sad when people are in the flesh that they cannot

*understand," said one visitor. "They are materialists who
cannot realise that none of it matters. It is only a stage set. No
one can go on when the curtain comes down."*

This is the difference between ignorance and knowledge.
Our task is always to ensure that knowledge spreads and
extends its boundaries all the time. With knowledge you can
face life and understand. With ignorance you are dwelling in
darkness.

It is very, very sad for us, particularly when we desire
only to help, that we find people are surrounded by a wall of
ignorance, prejudice and self-created superstition that cannot
be broken down because they are simply not ready. Truth
cannot penetrate that thick wall. It is sad because the ones they
love here cannot reach them either. For a time there is sorrow
on both sides of the veil. There is no need to shed tears for
those who leave your world. By recognising and accepting this
fact you do not hold them back. You do not create a barrier.
You enable the correct adjustments to be made to your mind
and spirit.

*This answer led a circle member to comment: "It is human
for us to be sad when a certain way of life has ended. Therefore,
even though we are sad, we are not grieving in a sense because
we know it is only, for a time."*

Those who come to my world recognise that death is a step
upward and they have earned their release. It – gives them
the opportunity to express latent gifts, to perform services that
they could not have done and to be more alive than ever was
possible before. Of course there is a tinge of sadness whenever
a break comes in your world. But recognition of the fact that
there is no sadness with the one who is promoted should help
to remove as much as possible of that tinge of sorrow. We must
always set an ideal for you to achieve.

The guide was then asked, "If two people love each other

and one is left in our world, would it be true to say that heaven is where the loved one is?"

Yes, as long as you recognise that it is a shared and not a divided loving. You cannot isolate love from its beloved.

Earth is only a temporary dwelling place. There can be no physical immortality. Recognising that there must come a time when you leave the earth means that in reality you should congratulate those who have reached it. And recognise also that you will join them and continue together in a land of greater light, beauty and wonder such as you can never appreciate on earth.

Another circle member said: "We have to consider this from our physical point of view. It is a period of waiting, but with ever-growing activity. We have to continue. It is very, very difficult."

Why should spiritual truths be difficult when considered from a physical viewpoint?

"Because we are physical beings, Silver Birch was told.

But primarily you are spiritual beings with physical bodies. The spirit is the greater and the physical the lesser. So in the light of the knowledge you possess you must make the right adjustment. All the things worth while must be difficult. If it were easy to earn spiritual prizes they would not be worth having.

Chapter Five

FROM BIRTH TO BEYOND—2

IT is very hard for me to convey to you what life in our world is really like. You have no knowledge of the infinite richness of the life in the world of spirit. There is no beauty anywhere, no majestic scenery, nothing you have visualised that can compare in its grandeur and in its infinite variety to that which can be seen in our world.

There can be no more inspiring way in which to begin this chapter which examines in detail life in the Beyond. The following questions and answers give valuable insights into the many facets of the spirit world which, says the guide, "is an example of the perfect operation of the perfect plan. You will find that nothing is left to chance."

How do people communicate with one another in the after-life?

When you come to our world you do not have physical bodies. You have their replicas, but you do not have speech. Except in the comparatively lower realms you realise there is a superior method of communication, mind to mind direct, without the necessity of using language which is a very clumsy substitute for thought. Thought is superior to language.

Similarly you do not consume food or drink because you do not have physical bodies that require to be sustained in this fashion. You do not want protein because no physical growth is required. You have spiritual bodies whose nourishment comes from the conditions where you live.

There is an eternal sun, no darkness, so you do not require

sleep. You are spiritually naked in the sense that nothing can be concealed. You are known for what you are, with pretence, substitution and camouflage being impossible.

Your level of communication is established only with individuals who are spiritually where you are. It cannot be. higher because you are not ready for anything that is spiritually upward until you evolve. You can descend spiritually because you are superior to those comparatively lower. So your communication is direct. What you think is known, just as equally you know what others think. There is no problem.

You live in this country and speak its language. When you meet a foreigner who does not speak English you cannot communicate because the language is different. But for thought no language is required, Thought communication is rapid. It presents no difficulties for us.

I am fed, if that is the right word, when I control this instrument, by others who give me thoughts, pictures, images or symbols that I have learned to translate into your language. It has taken a long time. I have to find the words in the medium's vocabulary, even sometimes those which he has forgotten but exist. When I am not using this instrument I have access to all your literature. I can find, if I need it, what your greatest masters have written and choose whatever I think may be suitable when the occasion arises. But when I leave this instrument I do not have to go through the laborious process of translating thought into your words.

How do you recognise one another?

We recognise individuals because we have spiritual eyes. We are not blind.

Here another sitter commented, "Our sight is physical."

You do not see with your eyes, neither do you hear with your ears. The perception is done with your mind via your brain. If your brain were not functioning and your mind inactive, every ray of light that touched your eyes would mean nothing to you and every vibration that reached your ears would be meaningless.

It is the mind which gives comprehension once the brain has acted as receiver. The eye does not have the ability to see. It only has the means of picking up radiations of light. It is like the lens of a camera. It is functioning automatically without awareness of what it is doing. Awareness comes from the mind when the brain has received the impression. If you damage the brain, then you will not see anything through your eyes because comprehension would be absent.

Next he was asked, "What do you actually see when you recognise somebody?"

We see human forms; they have heads; they have bodies.

You said you do not have a body.

Not a physical body; we have a spiritual body.

So it is a spirit body you see which you naturally recognise.

Of course. We are not all the same; we are different in our world.

The interrogation continued: "You were talking of reading books. Is that in the form of thought?"

We have duplicates of everything. There are libraries in which we have duplicates of everything that has been written in your world. We look at this literature, study it when necessary and acquire knowledge. We have access to music and to art. We have access to everything that is known in your world.

Another circle member asked, "At what state of earthly life do you see spirit forms?"

This depends on the level of awareness on which you are functioning at the time. The difference between your world and ours is that you can meet people at different levels of development. In our world you are restricted to the level which you have attained. The spirit body will be more mature the higher you are evolved. Growth in our world is towards maturity. Thus the old who come here become younger and the young become older because they are maturing.

Do you recognise the face?

Of course we have faces.

"Why do we have faces.?" the guide was asked.

Because individuality is the hallmark of every soul. No two souls can be alike; not even twins are the same spiritually. The process of attaining perfection, which in itself is infinite, does not mean you become faceless and formless. You attain a greater individuality, a growing spiritual maturity and an increasing light radiates from your being. As you ascend in this scale you find there are beings with such light that the radiance can almost dazzle you.

You have heard me say that when I leave your world and return to the inner spheres, I encounter some of the beings who belong to what may be called the hierarchy. These are all individuals. They have not discarded individuality. They have developed to the stage where imperfections are few and flawlessness is part of their being.

Why do we need bodies when we pass over to your world?

Because the spirit must have some form through which to manifest, to cohere, to express itself in individual fashion. Spirit, *per se*, has no individual forms. Spirit is life. But life to be manifested has to assume form whether it be human, animal, vegetable, flower, whatever it may be. Spirit could not be identified or recognised until it manifests in some form.

Does spirit hold its form for ever?

Yes.

I think you said a spirit entity on your side could not contact anybody who is at a greater stage of development. If this is so, is there any special dispensation when you personally meet the illumined ones?

No, if you will forgive me for saying so, I am merely returning to my natural state. I was asked to serve and I agreed. Naturally, to do so, I had temporarily to forfeit whatever I had. So I have the experience, which is similar to yours, that I am familiar with the polarity to which I frequently refer. I hope I am better for it.

It is very difficult to convey the totality of spirit life because we are confronted with a barrier of language and dimension. With music, for example, we have octaves of sound which are beyond the capability of any earthly instruments to register. With painting we have colours and beauty that you cannot imagine. There are not those on earth who are able to register or depict them. Even the greatest inspiration received in your world is only an infinitesimal fragment of what exists.

Said a visitor, "It cannot be easy for us to appreciate what the spirit world is like."

It is very difficult, but preparation is made in your sleep. Then you leave the physical body, "die" temporarily and gradually accustom yourselves to the spirit life. Otherwise, when the break with earth finally comes, it could be so difficult that it would take a long time for you to be conditioned to the new life. It is all in your subconscious minds what you have learned in your nocturnal excursions to our world. One day it will become your consciousness and thus it will not be so strange for you.

The circle's tallest member said: "Could I ask a question about size? Does a six foot person always remain at that height?"

Do you have a personal interest in this question? The answer is yes, because the physical body is the counterpart of the spiritual one. Size has no relevance to spiritual development. You can be a physical giant and a spiritual pygmy.

Is there a language problem at the beginning?

Yes, if you are dealing with what one might call astral spheres, that is, comparatively speaking, that part of the spirit world which is closest to earth. It is populated by people who hardly have any spiritual awareness. They still use language because they think it necessary.

If someone speaks English and another French, do they communicate with thought?

Of course. Thought has no language. Language is the vehicle for translating thought into words. You must try to realise that in our world thought is the reality and the physical is shadowy.

If you live in a non-physical world, is it the same for all who dwell in it, or is it one you, create by thought? If I were in it, would I see the same or a different world?

It depends where you were.

If we were together, would it be a creative world of my mind?

Not exactly. If you were where I am now, that is, we were on a similar level of being, then you would see what

I am seeing and you would experience what I am experiencing. As to what that world in which I now live, and which if you were with me would share, is made of is another matter. It is hard to convey in language, which is only an attempt to clothe pictures, ideas and symbols so that you can have some appreciation of the reality behind.the language.

We start by saying that life is spirit. Our world, like yours, exists because of spirit. Spirit is infinite and thus has endless manifestations. What is thought?

The visitor replied, "Thought is something that is a product of my mind, whatever my mind may be."

Is it real?

I think that possibly thought could be made real. I do not think in its beginning it is real.

But when you think you know you are thinking.

Yes, I think that you can make a thing positive.

So you are aware you are thinking. But you cannot see, hear, weigh or measure thought. There are no physical means of measurement. Yet thought is responsible for everything you do because it is the precursor to action. Without it there would be no action.

What you think in your world materialises as a physical action. What we think in our world materialises as a spiritual reality and is real to us just as your physical world is real to you. It is a matter of comparison. On our plane of being thought is as real as matter is on your sphere of existence.

A circle member joined in the discussion by saying: "Independent of people's thinking, in a physical world there is an objective reality, there are hills that all can see. In the spirit world is there such an objective reality independent of what people are thinking?" To this the visitor added, "We are sitting in this room – and we are aware of it."

But your awareness is different in every case. Life in our world is on varying levels of being, not in isolation, but merging into one another. Thus on one plane of being, objective reality, in the term that you use it, is the same for all who are there. They have hills, mountains, rivers, streams, birds, flowers and trees which are real.

In addition every individual has the power to create reality for himself by his thoughts. He can build out of the very plastic material of thought what he requires and which will, to use a comparative term, solidify and become real.

Having said this, could your world be physical?

It could, depending on how you define the word.

As my body is, composed of matter. When I die, could it be that my etheric body could also, be composed of matter with a higher speed of atomic revolution? Hence I can see it just as we are told we can speed up the atoms.

These are words. When you say "physical" and "matter," these terms must be defined. In a sense you can say that our world is composed of spiritualised matter, but it is not matter as you understand it. You speak about your physical body, but, as you say, it is composed of atoms.

Those atoms are composed of subdivisions. They have names for them, protons, electrons and neutrons. All these can be subdivided until you reach the stage where instrumentation takes you no further. You are aware that the dynamic is not physical. So your matter is physical only in its appearance. Its solidity is deceptive.

You have many bodies manifesting at varying rates. When you slough off the physical body you take on the etheric counterpart, which you have always had, and express yourself through it because that has the proper rate of vibration to enable you to function. That is all as real to the etheric as your physical body is to you while you are on earth.

It is all a question of the plane on which you are functioning. When you dream that you are in a ship this is real whilst you are asleep. It is only when you wake that you say, "I dreamt," and the ship becomes shadowy. But if your life were an eternal dream then all dream life would be reality. It would be as physical to you in your dream state as earthly life is to you in your waking state.

How do you know that you are not dreaming now? For all you know you may be part of a concerted dream. For many of us in our world there are millions on earth who are dreaming because they have not awakened to spiritual reality. What it comes back to is the awareness that you are not your body. As I have said, you are not bodies with spirits, you are spirits with bodies. It is a distinction with a very great difference.

A circle member asked, "Would you add to it that we are not personalities?"

No, only temporarily whilst you are on earth. A personality is the mask that you wear for your earthly existence. When earthly existence is over the mask is discarded.

I have a theory that the spirit progresses to perfection by way of manifesting through physical forms of different species ending with man. Is that right? Is it an idea I should pursue, or do you know if I am on the wrong track?

Do you mean that the individual spirit has been expressed through all forms of life before reaching its apex in man?

Yes.

This is not as an individual in the sense that I understand individuality. It is individual, say, when it animates a dog or a cat, but it is not individual in the sense when it animates a flower. The spirit is there wherever life is expressed. Spirit is life and life is spirit. You as spirit have always existed. In your present embodiment you became individualised from the moment of conception.

The evolution of you as an individual will continue in all forms of being. The higher you evolve the more individualised you become, but not in the sense of personality as you have it on earth. That is very difficult to understand. The purpose of evolution is to achieve perfection, but its attainment is an infinite process. As you progress and eliminate one imperfection you become aware of another that has to be expunged, and so the process goes on for ever.

What you must.try to realise is that there is a very big difference between personality and individuality. Personality is the extent of individuality expressed through a physical body. It is one of the forms that individuality has of manifesting while you are on earth.

But individuality has many other forms not restricted to the personality shown on earth. It is these other aspects that will continue to be unfolded as you leave earth behind and evolve in higher states of being. The more individualised .you become the less of personality there will be. The higher you go in the scale of spiritual values the less form is there such as you understand it when you look at bodies. It is difficult to find words to express all that is involved.

Our world is composed of people who come from your world. If you did not send us unevolved souls, we would have no trouble from them. You send millions who are unprepared, unfitted and ignorant. It is much more difficult to teach an adult the. lessons he should have learnt in school. You are subject to the whole range of spirit influence from the lowest to the highest. But you attract only those at the spiritual stage you have reached. Evil can be attracted only by evil. Saintliness will always attract saintliness. That is how the natural law operates.

Do not blame us for the existence of millions of souls many of whom are unaware of the fact that they are dead physically and almost dead spiritually. That is the work you have to do in your world, to prepare people for the life that inevitably awaits them when death comes to their. physical bodies.

The world of spirit has no geographical existence. I hear people talk of seven spheres as if we have a map. It is a graduated existence into which one sphere blends and merges into the other all the time. As you cast off imperfections you evolve to the sphere for which you are spiritually ready.

There comes a stage in your development when you are so aware of spiritual truths and do not require a comparison to understand or appreciate them. There is a stage even in earthly evolution when you achieve awareness and knowingness that cannot be measured by any intellectual content. That is what you achieve in our world when you do not require comparisons of opposites to find the reality.

We have had so many instances of planning in the spirit

*world which shows itself to us. How does that operate? Is there
a planner in chief somewhere who co-ordinates these things?*

There are brotherhoods, as we call them, each with a leader.
And at the head is the Nazarene who is still concerned with the
events in the development of your world. There are what you
would describe as conferences. You know that I withdraw to
go to the inner spheres when these conferences-they are really
councils-are held to check what has happened and to ensure
co-ordination.

There is a master plan and we all play our parts in it. I wish
it were possible-alas it is not-for you to be made aware of the
evolved beings in our world who, because of their evolution,
are concerned with the events of your earth. Others are
concerned with life in other forms of being, but the aspect on
which I am engaged is the one which deals with the people in
your world.

It is a perfect plan because perfection is responsible for
its creation, but ensuring it is fulfilled involves so many
considerations that it must of necessity be done very slowly.
Such questions as your free will, your karma, your destiny and
the choice you have made are all involved. These require a
perfect balance to ensure there will be progress, not necessarily
in a straight line because it cannot always follow that direction.
You should feel that you are helping to shape some of the
infinite processes of creation towards their divine fulfilment
in your world.

We are all highly privileged to participate, in however small a
measure, in helping that overall plan in its fulfilment according
to its grand design. Because of that I can say you need have
no fear of what the morrow will bring forth. Whatever the
difficulty, the obstacle, the handicap, the opposition, whatever
the stupidity, the ignorance and superstition you may encounter,
all will be divinely well because truth is on the march and none

can prevent it from attaining its goal. So hold your heads high and know that the power which is behind us is greater than any that can be encountered in your world.

This statement brought questions from circle members. The guide explained that some evolved beings who are part of the hierarchy he mentioned are not necessarily those who were once humans on earth. He could not add anything to what he had said about resuming his status. As to the plan, this was conceived in the past as part of an overall design. He appreciated all this was not easy to grasp.

The higher you climb in the scale of spiritual values the more difficult it becomes to explain it in your earthly language. We are dealing with spiritual contents. Language, only a clumsy means of interpretation, is limited in its definition because it cannot encompass what is outside normal appreciation.

He was asked, "Are there many higher spheres than those you speak about?"

Yes.

Are they continuous?

Yes, they are infinite.

Are they steps going up into the beyond?

Call them steps if you like.

Do the beings you mention have the ability to express themselves?

They are individuals; they are conscious; they are not automatons; they are radiant; they are the masters, the hierarchy, the representatives of the Great Spirit in our world.

Were they all humans?

No. If you read your Bible it mentions angels and archangels.

Does that mean there were always spirit beings?

There is no being anywhere who is not spirit.

I thought everybody had to have a span of our planet.

No. Your world is one of many in a vast multitude of worlds. It is not compulsory for every being to have inhabited your earth. There is an overall plan, comprehensive, all-inclusive in which nothing is excluded and nobody forgotten.

There are stars beyond the stars that you can see. There are planets beyond the planets, and worlds beyond the worlds that are known to you. The cosmos is so vast that it is infinite.

With no beginning and end?

Spirit has no beginning and no end. Spirit always was and will be. Read your Bible. The Nazarene said, "Before Abraham was I am."

Can we progress eventually to the spheres in which our friends are, and then be with them always?

If you reach their level of attainment, of course you can. These matters are self-determined. You occupy the sphere, stage or state of being that you have spiritually reached. All those on that level are of similar unfoldment. You get the answer to the question when you have reached their spiritual stage. Progress is always possible because it is eternal, a striving towards perfection..

What happens when two people love each other and one is spiritually much higher than the other? Would the one less spiritual have to wait before he or she joined the other?

It is usually the other way round. The one who has the greater attainment will wait because love is involved.

Would you say something about the process of dying and arriving in the spirit world?

It is the sloughing off of the physical body as the spirit body gradually emerges. It is never a painful process. There may be some physical reactions when there is illness or disease. If the transition is not a simple one, then the equivalent of your doctors stand by. They help those who love this individual to accomplish his or her birth into our world until the cord connecting spirit and matter severs itself and separation is assured for all time.

The question of awakening is the next to be considered. This depends on the degree of awareness that the newcomer possesses. If completely ignorant of the fact that life continues after earthly death, or if so indoctrinated with false ideas that understanding will take a long time, then there is a process of rest equivalent to sleep.

That continues until it is self-determined that the time for realisation has come. This can be short or long, as measured by your duration of time. It depends upon the individual. Those with knowledge have no such problems. They step out of the world of matter into the world of spirit and adjustment is speedy. When awakening comes it is a moment of supreme joy because it brings recognition of all the loved ones who have been waiting for it to occur.

Could you tell us what is the span of the etheric body? We have an etheric body when we pass over. How long does it last?

How long is a piece of string? You cannot measure this body. It is a spiritual not a physical development. You have many bodies; you can call them astral, etheric and spirit. You manifest in the body which is capable of expressing the state you have reached. When you evolve to another stage, you shed that body like the caterpillar does. You express yourself in the form suitable for your latest development. This is how it works. It is infinite progression.

What is our true self, not the physical or the astral?

These are words. All words, being physical, can never convey the totality of that which is beyond language. There are no words that can truly interpret what the spirit is. The spirit is not material; it is not three-dimensional; it is not located geographically anywhere. It does not occupy space as your body does. Spirit is invisible, inaudible and intangible so far as your palpable material senses are concerned.

Spirit is the reality; spirit is the life force; spirit is the dynamic. Spirit is part of the Great Spirit.

So you are a triune being. You have a physical body, you have a spirit body and you have a soul. You can change the words around and call it a soul body. It does not matter; you are only trying to find words. The soul is the divine spark, that part of the Great Spirit that is within you.

You are not your body; your body is not you. Your spirit body is the means by which you will express yourself once the physical body has dissolved and been returned to nature.

The true self is not an exterior, the surface, the shell, but the kernel, the real nut, the heart, the soul, the life, the God that is within you. Spirit, being infinite, has many manifestations and gradations. There is a series of bodies of the spirit given various names like astral and etheric, but these are only manifestations of the one spirit. Do not be bothered by semantics. Words are only tools.

At this stage Silver Birch answered submitted questions. The first were: "How far does the similarity between the physical and etheric bodies extend? What could be the point of gastric juices, an auditory system, or leg muscles in a spirit body? Shall we still have the sense of touch?"

There would be no point. You have an etheric body which reproduces its physical counterpart, but this does not contain muscles, gastric juices or an auditory system. The etheric counterpart is the intervening envelope for the spirit to manifest and function efficiently through the physical body. When death comes, the etheric has served its primary purpose as the vehicle for the soul to continue its next phase. The etheric is sloughed off and another body replaces it. The processes of refinement require more spiritual vehicles for expression. You can have many bodies.

If we have many bodies, what happens at death? Do they fall of one by one?

As you evolve you slough off the different bodies.

Do you mean to say we go on dying?

Yes, not spiritually, only as a means of expression.

After we pass on we slough of the etheric. Is that another death?

Yes, it is just like getting rid of the physical body when it has served its purpose.

Do we die many times?

Of course, but it is a good thing that you do. It means you are progressing.

Eventually shall we become pure spirit with no body at all?

I doubt if you achieve that stage, but you get closer to it all the time.

Surely that is the whole point of spiritual evolution?

The whole purpose of life itself is evolution, development, growth, attainment. As you evolve, so automatically you discard the body which has served its purpose and assume the one that is fitted for your stage of evolution.

In a way it is only like on earth where we have several skins.

And you have new bodies every seven years. You, the spirit, can never disappear.

Are there opportunities in the spirit world for service?

Oh, far more than you face on earth. We have problems such as you cannot possibly realise. We have to deal with millions of souls in many parts of the spiritual universesick souls, young souls, forgotten souls, lonely souls, malformed souls, ignorant souls. Have we got problems? We have them because you send them to our world.

Are people in the spirit world limited or is the universe wide open to them? Can they travel? Can they explore?

Of course they can, if they have earned the right to explore. It is a question of development. There has to be a purpose.

Replying to another comment Silver Birch said:

It is very hard for me to convey to you what life. in our world is really like. I speak truthfully when I tell you that there is so much to explore on this side. You have no knowledge of the infinite richness of the life in the world of spirit. There is no beauty anywhere, no majestic scenery, nothing you have visualised that can compare in its grandeur and in its infinite variety to that which can be seen in our world.

Am I right in saying that many individuals in the next world have more or less denied themselves the right to explore by continuing the work they did here? The guide said:

There are many who were doctors in your world who prefer to use their earthly knowledge plus their added power to help the sick. That is the hall-mark of spiritual unfoldment.

Here a remark by a circle member caused Silver Birch to say:

There are laws which regulate everything. You will find that nothing is forgotten or overlooked. I always marvel at the perfection of the natural law and its methods of governing.

My sister was mentally deficient due to instruments used at her birth. She was very deformed in every way. How will I recognise her in the next world? Would she have this deformed appearance? Why did she have to live 40 years in this deformed state?

If we remove the question from its personal aspect and deal with the principle it would be easier. There is no individual in your world who is exempt from the law of compensation or even retribution. Always there is a stage when the spiritual account is balanced, and the two aspects, the debit and the credit, are even. Any deficiencies in your world are compensated in ours.

Deformity is a physical imperfection. You cannot have a

deformed mind or spirit. What you can have is an immature mind and spirit due to the fact that they have not had the opportunities for manifesting because of an undeveloped brain. On passing into our life, such an individual is possibly at the evolution that a child would have attained, but there is no damage to the mind or to the spirit.

As to why it happens, this is much more difficult--cause and effect, wrong instruments used, mishandling and the body is affected and the brain made incapable of being the instrument of manifestation and registration that it should. Why should this be so? It may be a karmic condition. I cannot answer a personal question. I can deal only with the principles involved.

A sitter said, "This person wants to know how will she recognise her sister in the next life."

Recognition is not so difficult as is supposed. The one who comes to our world is watched over by those who are close to him or her. They will know when the time of passing has come and be able to greet them. A spirit entity can manifest temporarily in any form which will make recognition possible. The child who has been in our world for many years, according to physical measurement, can appear temporarily as a child when the mother comes to our life. So that is no problem.

Can our loved ones see us in either spiritual or physical form, or in both?

This is a little. difficult because it depends on the talent possessed by people in our world. Generally speaking they see your spirit body more than your physical body unless they have a special talent, which is the equivalent of the clairvoyance that mediums exercise. I cannot at this moment see anything physical in this room, but I can see the spirit bodies of those who are present.

At the time of passing into your world is there some organisation for people's loved ones to be so advised?

No organisation is necessary because those who love you are with you. They are aware of your passing long before you are. They stand there waiting to help in the transition. Love is the greatest attracting force in the universe. Those who love you cannot be separated from you.

A visiting medium asked the guide to answer an intriguing question. That day her mediumship enabled a husband, who had passed on only a month earlier, to return to his wife. His communication included statements describing what he did in the mornings, afternoons and evenings. Were such periods of time experienced? Silver Birch said:

That happens in the early stages of coming to our world because the spirit has not adjusted itself to the new environment. The lower planes, the astral ones, are in many respects a duplicate of earthly existence. This is a divine provision to enable newly-arrived inhabitants to acclimatise themselves, otherwise it would be too difficult for them.

So you get people, like the one you mentioned, who still think that life, even in our world, consists of mornings, afternoons and evenings. Because they think like that it happens in this fashion. Our world is one where thought is reality. Until realisation dawns this temporary stage continues. Besides, in such a case the partner will want to help the one left behind and would have no desire to progress any higher spiritually.

We have gardens, houses, lakes, seas and oceans. They exist because ours is a real world. We do not inhabit a formless creation. We are still human beings, though without physical bodies. But we enjoy the beauties of nature and have a radiance. of living that is beyond description because there are no means of conveying it.

It is natural to live in a home, but the home here is the one you have created by your life on earth. It is natural to have gardens. If you think they require tending, then you do so.

Ultimately you learn it is not necessary and that provision has been made for them to receive all the attention necessary for their sustenance. Without such provision, transition from the earth to . the world of spirit would create a tremendous shock.

Spirit life is graduated, with each sphere, plane or expression blending and shading into the next one higher in the evolutionary sense but not in geographical location. As the soul progresses and fits itself for higher states of being, so automatically it occupies those states. All this is an example of the perfect operation of the perfect plan. You will find that nothing is left to chance.

The sick in spirit when they come here go to hospitals where they receive the necessary attention. The children who are, so to speak, orphans in our world because their parents are in yours, have foster-mothers to care for them. Sometimes they were related to them by ties of blood, but in other cases there is a spiritual kinship which is the attraction. Provision is made for every circumstance because the natural law omits nothing and nobody.

The whole purpose of earthly life is to provide a variety of experiences that will enable people, at some stage, to become aware of the existence of that which is below the surface. I am sure the operation of natural law is such that this opportunity is afforded to every normal being. Otherwise it must be that the Great Spirit has neglected or removed its power from some individuals, and that is not possible. The very act of a birth of a spirit into your world means that potentially this child has all the awareness that can be expressed, and opportunities are given for it to happen.

Chapter Six

ON SOCIAL PROBLEMS

I AM in favour of people being permissive as long as they permit themselves to do the right thing. You are all endowed with a divine monitor. You call it conscience. It tells you when you are right or wrong.

There can be no more fitting quotation with which to begin this chapter which examines some of today's moral, ethical and social problems. The last decade or so has seen a revolution in society's ideas which its inhabitants either applaud or abhor.

Silver Birch was asked this two-part question by a circle member: "There are a lot of people who are worried and troubled about what is happening in our society at the moment. How should a Spiritualist conduct himself or herself in these times?" The guide replied:

Those with knowledge should never allow fear to effect any lodgement within them. Your world has had many troubles. It will have troubles until spiritual principles are the foundation on which orders of society are built. To try and erect these on a materialistic basis is equivalent to building on quicksand. You cannot have peace without while there is war within. How can there be co-operation when hatred, violence, enmity, greed and sloth are the expressions of too many people?

Love is the fulfilling of the law. You must love one another because you recognise that every individual in your world is your spiritual brother or sister, and that the whole human family consists of spiritual kith and kin. This is what the Great

Spirit has done by implanting into every being a portion of its own divinity so that the chain of the spirit in which you are all links girdles the whole of your world.

At present there is no recognition of this eternal fact that primarily you are spiritual beings none of whom can live in isolation from others, that your evolution is bound up with one another, that you advance or retreat collectively.

This is your responsibility. I have always said that. knowledge brings responsibility as to how it is to be employed. Once you are aware of spiritual truths, once you are familiar with the workings of the power of the spirit, you should have no fear of today or the morrow.

No harm will befall your spirit. If you live according to what you know and what has been revealed to you, you will come through unsinged no matter what the fire. You cannot be spiritually hurt or crushed by whatever happens in your world. You have all had evidence in your own lives of what the power of the spirit can do when the conditions are right.

Unfortunately those who are aware of these vital truths are the few and not the many. The majority think that power resides in matter, in force, in domination, in tyranny, in slavery. But all the children of the Great Spirit are born to be free in body, mind and spirit.

Gradually as these truths infiltrate and permeate everywhere, the children of earth will live in greater liberty and a brighter lustre will be their everyday existence. You have not come to the end of the story in this land or in any other lands. The divine power of evolution will slowly and gradually reveal itself. People on earth may block, impede and delay, but they cannot alter the divine will.

If they could overcome the will of the Great Spirit then the earth would have crumbled a long time ago. Spirit is superior to matter. The divine spirit is the overruling power. I always say, lift up your hearts, hold your heads high, there is nothing to fear in your world, or in ours for that matter. You will come through.

Should we not encourage our speakers to concentrate more on attacking what is known to be wrong, such as the colour bar, encouraging hate of various nations, cruelty to animals and children?

Yes, as long as you stress that the reason why you attack these cruelties, misunderstandings and discriminations is because they are spiritually wrong apart from being physically wrong. You have a unique attitude towards these problems because you are aware of spiritual realities.

Because man is a spirit he must have a body fit enough to be its temple. Therefore his mind must have the education that is essential to equip that temple. His body must have the right conditions, the right home, the right clothing, the right food, because it is spiritually necessary for this to be so.

It is spiritually wrong to be cruel to animals. It is spiritually wrong to have race or colour discrimination. The soul has no colour. It is not yellow, red, black or white. If you stress the spiritual aspect, then you are emphasising the most important contribution you can make.

My point is that we should protect ourselves against brainwashing attempted by all the media that teach us nothing but hate.

If you have spiritual awareness you cannot hate your spiritual brother..

I think we who know more have to help.

Yes, the greater the knowledge, the greater the responsibility.

And when we're aware, to be tolerant.

Tolerance is the essence of spirituality. If there is bigotry, there is no spirituality.

It's all very well saying be tolerant, I agree, but one must define what one means by tolerance in relation to a concrete world. We certainly shouldn't be tolerant of cruelty or evil in any form.,

You must also define evil. The whole purpose of earthly life is to develop your spiritual nature so that you are ready for the next stage beyond what is called death. You will have an increasing degree of awareness. As your spiritual nature unfolds and advances, so automatically you will become more tolerant and more compassionate to others. That does not mean to say you must be tolerant towards evil, cruelty, or wickedness of any kind. It is a tolerance towards others because you realise they are less informed than you are. Often they are doing things through sheer ignorance because they are unaware of the implications of their actions.

That is where your tolerance is necessary. But it is not a tolerance that should accept evil and disregard it. That is not toleration, but ignoring the obvious. -Tolerance involves awareness, and a readiness to serve wherever you can.

Toleration comes from love and loving kindness. When you love individuals you tolerate their faults. I think toleration, which means love, is what the world lacks now. And if we could combine the two, we would have more elevation.

I agree with you. Your Bible says that love is the fulfilling of the law. Love is the law, the law of the Great Spirit, because the Great Spirit is love. And when you reflect the Great Spirit you are expressing love. By love I mean compassion, the desire to serve, to sacrifice, to help, to do all within your power for those who are less fortunate than you are. This is the love that ignores self and wants to do what it can for someone who needs the service you can give.

Some people maintain that society today has never been more immoral. Is that the view of the spirit world? They

*instance what happened 50 to 100 years ago. when children
were sent to work, cleaning chimneys, etc. Silver Birch said:*

What is meant by immoral? Some things you regard as moral
we would regard as highly immoral. It depends on your outlook.
To me morality is that ideal which infuses you with the idea of
acting always according to the highest principles of which you
are aware. This is to be kind, helpful, compassionate.

It is not to inflict hurt or injury on another; not in any way to
impede the progress of another; to do nothing that causes you
shame or a later knowledge that you have behaved in a fashion
that is inconsistent with the truths you have received.

That is the morality I understand, that I would teach to
others. As to whether your world is more or less moral must
depend on your interpretation of morality. In some respects it
is essentially economically and spiritually better; in others it is
not so because evolution does not move in a straight line.

*We are told we live in a world that is materialistic. Surely
in today's society one has to be materialistic to a degree to
provide security for one's family. If one is too Spiritualistic it
could lead to financial hardship for one's family. Where does
one draw the line?*

Seek ye first the kingdom of God and heaven, and, all these
other things will be added unto you.

"Surely one can do both," it was suggested.

Of course. But if you have your priorities right, and are
spiritually aware, you will not neglect those dependent on you.
We have never taught you should avoid your responsibilities in
the physical world. You must have your priorities right and be
aware of your spiritual responsibilities as well as your physical
ones. Do not neglect the spirit, the mind or the body or seek to
cast away that for which you are responsible.

*Before examining the implications of abortion, here are
the guide's views on contraception. A guest explained it was*

a frank but very important question. Silver Birch had, he said, taught that "birth is a natural law. In that case is it wrong for people to practise birth control because they are interfering with the natural. law?"

Here is the spirit reply:

No, they are not. It is right for them to practise the physical control of birth if they decide to do so for reasons which they regard as good, be they economic, for health and various other factors. Motive decides these questions. If the motive is right then everything will fall into its proper place. There is nothing wrong with the practice of birth control when the motive is right. 'But there are millions who welcome the opportunities of coming together so that they can provide the beginning of a physical body for a life to function on earth.

When the subject of abortion was raised, the questioner wanted to know "at what point is it wrong?"

From the very moment it is done.

Even at the earliest?

The answer is from the very moment it is done it is wrong. Listen, you have no power to create life. You have power to transfer life. You have no right to destroy its expression. Abortion is akin to murder. From the moment of conception the spirit has incarnated into the woman's womb. When it is aborted it will continue to be a spiritual body, however immature, and grow and develop. You may have destroyed the means of physical expression, but you have not destroyed the spirit that was there. Abortion is interference with the embryonic spirit which is developing according to its natural growth. There are qualifications when the motive is right. That will always be taken into account.

I do not know of any evolved being in my world who favours abortion. But always there is the qualification that the motive must be taken into consideration. The act itself is condemned.

You do not create life. You should not therefore end the means by which it expresses itself. If those who practise abortion realised they were not merely getting rid of matter, but a living entity with whom one day they will be confronted, I think there would be fewer abortions. From the moment of conception, there is the beginning of an individual, who will never die and continue to grow in my world.

"It is a terrifying thought bearing in mind what is happening on earth," the guide was told.

It is a fact.

Will they incarnate when the time comes?

Yes, responsibility cannot be evaded. If the purpose of incarnation is for them to fulfil themselves and this is denied, they will return not once but many times if necessary.

A different visitor asked about people with complete brain damage who, though compared with cabbages, are kept alive by machines in hospitals. "Is keeping them alive altering the plan of the Great Spirit? What happens to their spirits? Are these still linked with the physical bodies? Are they asleep? Should they be released?" The guide answered:

The purpose of the earthly existence is that the spirit should equip itself for the greater life that awaits' it after physical death. The fulfilment of that purpose should be achieved if lives are lived in harmony with the natural law, so that when the time is ripe and the body has served its purpose, the spirit separates itself. As I have often said, the spirit should leave the body as the apple leaves the tree when it is ripe.

In the case of those you mention who have experienced brain damage, it must always be the motive of doctors to do all that lies in their power to maintain the life of their patient. In olden days the doctors took an oath that this would be the purpose of all their professional activity. It is never right spiritually for anyone in your world to interfere in that process of the operation of natural law, that the spirit should quit the body when the time is ripe. There is a qualification that when doctors accelerate that process, and their motive is unquestionably a good one, then you cannot blame them for what they do.

The patient suffering from the damage can be compared with a machine where the transmission is faulty because something has gone wrong with the dynamo or the motor. It can work only at a fraction of what should be its usual efficiency.

Because the brain is damaged, the mind, which you can call the brain of the spirit, is unable to express itself as it should. There is no damage to the mind because there is damage to the brain. If you have a typewriter and the keys are not working, it only means that the typist cannot use the machine. It does not mean that the typist has in any way been damaged.

The mind is handicapped. It lacks the development which it should have attained had there been a normal existence. So that when passing comes, the passing to our world, that soul is at a stage where it has to make up for what it has lost, almost like a child who comes to our life. But there is no damage spiritually as far as the individual is concerned.

As long as the spirit animates the body that link will be maintained. When the cord that connects the spirit to the body, just as there is a cord connecting the mother to the baby, is cut, this life is released. It is the spiritual life for the one who has died physically and the physical life for the one who has been born into your world.

The questioner commented, "We hear of people who are just passing on and they are kept alive by machines." Silver Birch told him:

This raises the question of euthanasia. One visitor wanted to know the spirit world's attitude. The guest said:

"We read reports of people involved in a car accident. They are taken to hospital. If they do not pass on they are left to live

as cabbages, unable to do anything for themselves. Why are
they left on earth when they cannot develop spiritually in such
a condition? Why cannot euthanasia be put into practice?"
The guide replied:
It says somewhere in your Bible, "The Lord giveth and the
Lord taketh away; blessed be the name of the Lord."
I quote these words because they are true. Life comes from
the Great Spirit. You cannot create life, neither can you destroy
it. You can provide the mechanism in which life will function.
You can destroy that mechanism, but the gift of life is not
yours. Life is the responsibility which is entrusted to you.

When it comes to judgement, beware of making assessments
based only on physical measurement. You cannot measure the
spirit with a physical yardstick. Your natural pity, sympathy,
mercy and compassion are aroused when you see an individual
reduced to what you call a cabbage. But the cabbage has a life
and a purpose to serve in your world otherwise it would not
be there.

A person is injured in an accident. His body is so mutilated
that its machinery is incapable of giving the spirit the fulness
of its expression. Do you regard this problem as physical or
spiritual? Spiritually there is a purpose to be served, a lesson to
be learned, an experience to be undergone. Physically it may
all seem motiveless. But until you can see with the eye of the
spirit, until you can understand eternal scales of values, your
judgement must of necessity be based on fallacies.

I am completely and utterly opposed to killing these
individuals, though the act is qualified by the motive in doing
so. This, however, is not the answer. Once you entrust to others
the decision as to when they shall kill, you are giving them a
power which they are all not capable of having. Nor should
they have the responsibility of this decision.

A circle member asked, "If a person is suffering, have not we some responsibility to relieve him of further suffering?"

If you are referring to illness, disease or infirmity, it is possible that conventional medicines cannot cure or improve the condition. But there are other forms of treatment which can and do produce beneficial results. The criterion must not be what the. medical verdict is. We must establish that first of all. We are all familiar with many cases where medical verdicts have been disproved and other healing forces have produced cures or betterment.

Suffering has its purpose. Suffering is essential because it is a means of touching the soul and calling into being the hidden forces that will or should enable the individual to be stronger in spirit and sometimes in body as a result. Suffering for many people is the catalyst that enables them to view the whole of life from a totally different standpoint.

Do not write off anybody as impossible of improvement. This is the wrong attitude. I know it is an adage in your world that where there is life there is hope. This is true. As long as the spirit inhabits that frame it is possible that it can stimulate recovery, reinvigorate, recharge and enable the body to function with some degree of efficiency. The natural law, if allowed to operate, will ensure that when the time is ripe the body will drop away because the spirit is ready for its departure.

The questioner said: "I have been in touch with a case of cancer. The pain is just beginning and it does seem wrong."

But pain can be alleviated. There are medical means of doing so. If pain is the problem, it can be dealt with. Even when conditions are intolerable I must insist this is not the final verdict so far as we are concerned. I would be false to everything I teach if I said that the final verdict is to be given by those whose minds are restricted to one set scale of discipline.

Another circle member pointed out, "In our experience we

have many cases of inoperable cancer where the pain has been taken away by spirit healing."

"Yes, I would agree," said the previous speaker, "but there are many where it is not."

"Perhaps the answer is that we should have a greater knowledge of spirit power, put more into operation so that there are reservoirs of it when these things happen."-"But this does not help the person."

The guide told him:

You can always give healing. You can always pray and help in that direction because the thought has great potency that can produce results. Never accept the pessimistic view of those who, intelligent though they may be, are earthbound in their outlook.

"It has very often been said that suffering ennobles a person," interposed the second circle member. "Often it does not happen." Silver Birch said:

I never say it automatically ennobles the individual, but it can do so because suffering is one of the inevitable experiences of earthly life that you must endure on earth. As you have often heard me say, sunshine and rain, storm and peace, you cannot have one without the other.

If your entire earthly existence is unalloyed happiness, then it would cease to be happiness because you would not realise it. You know it is happiness because you have had sorrow. Suffering is often the means to enable you to appreciate what your life is all about. It is through suffering, sorrow, illness, crisis and bereavement that spiritual eyes can be opened. To many people, these are the means by which they come to an understanding of eternal realities.

Unfortunately many people when they suffer become unhappy, bitter and narrow.

This is because they have no enduring foundation for their

existence. If your philosophy, religion and outlook are founded on a rock of knowledge, then, come what may, when the winds of adversity blow, you will not be disturbed. You will recognise them as part of the pattern, not the whole, but only a part.

The corollary would seem that suffering should go only to those people who have reached that stage of development where they can appreciate it.

You must take that up with the Great Spirit. All I can say is that having viewed life on many planes of being, the natural laws operate with exactitude and do not err.

Another member joined the discussion with: "There must be a number of people who do not want to die. If doctors were given the power to kill them, some of these people would be the last who would want it."

This is not a decision that they or the doctors should be called on to make. Let us face certain facts. The majority of doctors are materialistic in outlook. Their knowledge of medicines is founded on a materialism which has not recognised that man is a body, mind and a spirit. So far as the medical world is concerned, man is a body with a brain and perhaps a mind, but no recognition comes to the spirit. How can you therefore entrust the responsibility of such vital decisions to people who are completely ignorant of the most important matters in life?

Sometimes people sign a form saying if they are rendered incapable physically after an accident, they would wish to pass on.

That is a decision which they make of their free will.

What is the position if the doctor acts on this request?

There is no blame.

Does the law of cause and effect come into operation when a person passes of his own free will?

The law of cause and effect always comes into operation. Your birth is due to the operation of natural law. Your death should be due to the operation of natural law. If you choose to short-circuit, to interfere, then obviously you are breaking what should be a natural sequence and a price must be paid for it.

You have heard me say many times that death should come when the spirit is ready, just as the apple drops from the tree when it is ripe. If you pull the apple from the tree before it is ready, the fruit is not palatable. If the spirit is forced out of the body when it is not ready, then a penalty has to be paid. That is the law of cause and effect.

Your judgement is based purely on physical observation. The purpose of life is spiritual. It is not right for you to remove people from your world. You cannot see the whole picture. You can look only on the physical side. There is a time to be born and a time to die. It is all part of a natural law. You do not give life, you should not take it away. Life belongs to the Great Spirit.

With infinite wisdom the Great Spirit has devised the natural laws that ensure justice is meted out to every individual. If you try to judge eternity by this earthly fraction you will not succeed because you have no means of measuring the spirit or the reactions to it.

Some suffering is good for the soul. It tests its calibre. It calls into being latent strength. Steel can be forged only in the flame. Gold emerges only after crushing and refining.

There is a purpose in all that happens in your world. I understand your sympathies, but nothing happens by chance in your world. Besides, who is to decide these matters? Your doctors can be wrong, as they have been many times.

We often see things in reverse from you. Physical senility. can be spiritual birth. Your disorders we can often see as advances and your advances as disasters. To measure eternity with a physical yardstick will not give you any satisfactory answers.

Why does anybody suffer? Why do children suffer? Why do you have pain, illness, trouble and crisis? It is all part of the long story of your evolution.. In some cases you know before you come into earth that this is what you have accepted.

There would be no growth unless you were subjected to all the variety of experiences that provide the lessons you learn for your spiritual equipment. This in brief is the whole purpose of being.

I have said itt before. It is only in darkness that you find the light. If there were no darkness you would never know what light is. There are the principles of compensation and retribution. The Great Spirit is the perfect judge. The balance is always struck. The pages of the ledger show the right balance when the accounts have to be prepared. Continue to have sympathy, but try to realise there is an underlying purpose in all the seemingly sad and troublesome experiences.

In eternity a few hours or days are of little import. It is the effect on the soul that is important. As you probably know, very often you are-suffering more than the patient, who is getting only a mechanical reflex reaction and not feeling what you think is being felt.

What happens to the soul is the most important. I do not mean by that that you have to be impervious as to what happens to the body. The body is the means by which the soul expresses itself on earth. There is a constant reaction. The body affects the spirit and the spirit affects the body. But the superior is the spirit. The spirit is king and the body is the subject.

Drugs poured into a body will not hurt the spirit. They may for a while delay the final severance, but they cannot alter the law which determines that the spirit must be freed by death. You cannot, for example, by any drug or medication achieve physical immortality because that is controlled by the natural law.

Man-made death of a different type, suicide, arose after a questioner said: "You naturally, and quite rightly, condemn shortening of life by using external physical means. But it is possible for persons without using any external means to will themselves to die. Would you consider it a form of suicide?"

Nothing can change personal responsibility. The law of cause and effect is inexorable. Effect will always follow cause.

It may be that the individual welcomes the fact of passing because he believes in life after death. The body has become cumbersome. He so welcomes death that he would not endeavour to sustain the body by medical means when it becomes cumbersome.

Then the motive is the only important consideration. The motive will qualify the action.

Reports we receive of the condition of suicides in your world is that they are unhappy, disorientated and miserable. But of course they were in that condition before they committed suicide. Therefore it is natural they will be in the same condition when they pass from this world. What if a person committed suicide out of sheer joy and happiness?

Then the motive is selfish. You can't cheat the natural law. There are no exceptions. What you sow you must reap. There cannot be any other way. Your motive decides. Your conscience tells you what is right or wrong at the time. If you choose to equivocate, that is your responsibility.

An unusual aspect came when a guest said: "We are told by doctors that if people eat, drink and smoke to excess they are liable to kill themeslves. Are they committing a form of suicide or are deaths preordained?"

The answer is implicit in the question. If it is ordained, then whether it is suicide or not means it is predestined. So if it is ordained it would have to take place. It could be the soul is aware that it is ordained.

I can never make up my mind if deaths are already known when we are born, or whether we change them by our own actions.

Known to whom?

Possibly to ourselves or those we left behind on the Other Side.

It is known, but all cannot be revealed. The fraction of earth life over infinity is infinitesimal. What is above that line in the fraction, whatever the figure may be, is microscopic compared with what is below it. The smaller cannot include the larger; the larger can include the smaller. Whatever awareness there may be embodied in the recesses of the soul it cannot be expressed until it is ready for it to be done.

You have free will within relative conditions. You can change part of the tapestry, but not the pattern on which it is based. You have to work that out for yourselves. Every soul in your world is given the opportunity to put himself or herself right with the overriding power. None is condemned to a darkness unless it chooses to refuse the light. Motive is the paramount consideration for. all actions. Motive decides whether the action is right or wrong. You cannot cheat the law.

Lastly, here are the guide's views on an ever-present social, moral and spiritual problem, capital punishment:

I have never hesitated to say what I regard is spirit teaching that one murder does not justify another. The people of your world must distinguish between justice and revenge. To send any soul unprepared into our world may justify the lowest passions of humans in your world, but it accomplishes nothing. Justice should be done. By your world performing murder it has not increased by one iota its spiritual upward evolution. Instead it has descended and .indulged in "an eye for an eye and a tooth for a tooth." When passion usurps reason what follows cannot be right.

We must adhere to principles which we know are true because they are founded on the indisputable fact that life continues after physical death. You create more and more troubles by sending into our world people who are unprepared for it. In some cases the execution is performed on the wrong individual and justice is not done.

Life is sacred and is not yours to give or take away. Life is your responsibility. Life is not created by matter. Matter is created and sustained by life. Life is of the spirit; life emanates from the Great Spirit; life is divine. When you deal with life and its expressions you should always adopt the highest standards of mercy, compassion and sympathy. Make sure that your motive is right in whatever you do.

Chapter Seven

TO LIVE IN HARMONY

LOVE is the most potent force in the universe. With its almost magical qualities, seemingly insurmountable obstacles can be overcome and vanquished.

But everything in life has its opposites for a simple but oftforgotten reason: how, for example, could we know love without hate, happiness without suffering, company without loneliness?

This chapter collates Silver Birch's views on a range of human emotions and situations that probably affect all during their earthly sojourn. In short it is a blueprint for living life to its fullest, acting not on foolhardy optimism, but on the foundation that Survival conviction assures the right perspective in all matters.

Thus life's rich harvest can be gathered in spiritual peace and harmony – within and without.

What people in your world do not understand is the tremendous potency of love. Love is the greatest power in the universe. Love is the fulfilling of the law. Love is the obverse side of the coin of life. If there were no divine love there would be no life in the universe. Life exists in its multitudinous forms only because divine love is responsible for its creation. Where there is true human love it is a reflection of divine love. It has in essence, though not of course to the same degree, all the aspects of divine love.

Thus where there is love that cements two beings, and one is parted from the other by the death of the physical body, it acts as the attracting, magnetic, pulsating power. It enables the one in our world to break through all the difficulties and to make the conditions such that they can manipulate the atmosphere around you to ensure that what is best for you spiritually shall be accomplished. And what is best for you spiritually in the end is best for you materially.

At one circle a young medium commented: "People use the word `love' like a parrot, but they do not love. People, like yourself, come back with so much knowledge. But those who read it do not always act on it. There is something lacking which I do not understand." The reply came:

It means they have a lot to learn. Sometimes I think the word "love" is the most misused one in your world. Love is expressed in service, mercy, goodness, compassion, kindliness. Love means helping wherever you can. Love means forgetting self Love seeks nothing for itself but only to redeem itself by serving others. All you can do is to set the example and hope that others may follow.

I am always grateful for love. Love is what we offer your world. When on earth love replaces hatred, compassion drives out cruelty, and mercy and tolerance are the natural outlook of the majority, then you will have rid your planet of many of those foul excrescences that erode all the time.

If there were love, the blots, stains, cancers and all the foul things in your world would be abolished. Greed, avarice and selfishness, all the products of materialism, are responsible for the violence, ugliness and squalor that unfortunately are too rampant in your world. That is why we strive to enunciate these spiritual truths and principles which, if put into practice, enable people to find themselves and change their lives and as a result change the world in which they live.

There is no other way. It cannot be changed by conversion to a creed or doctrine, by legislation in parliaments, though these can provide some amelioration to physical conditions. It can be done only through self-regeneration. Then the spirit comes into its own and its divine qualities are expressed all the time.

A woman visitor said: "My son has married somebody who believes in women's liberation. I do not know whether that has percolated into your sphere."

It did not have to percolate.

This is the younger generation who have quite different ideas from ours. Do you think the present rumblings of women's liberation are perhaps the promise of something much better to come in the shape of a higher form of marriage with freedom and a higher kind of constancy, not enforced, not selfish, exclusive of love, but unselfish including others?

Let us analyse these questions and comments, and start at the beginning. What is love? If it is selfish it is not love because love cannot be selfish. Love of necessity means sacrifice, service, compassion, helpfulness, so it cannot be selfish.

As for constancy, love, when it is love, and thus an expression of divine love, must be constant. If it is not constant it ceases to be love. When you come to discuss liberation this really turns on what you believe you are to be liberated from.

Bondage.

If there is love there is no bondage.

But the young people think there is a lot of bondage in marriage.

They are wrong. If there is love they cannot be bound except a willingness to be bound to one another by the natural attracting power of love. Who would want to be separated when love has joined them together? So there is no bondage where there is love.

Of course we favour liberation, not only for women, not only for men, not only for children, but also for the animals in your world who are in bondage. We believe in liberation because the spirit should achieve freedom wherever it can and not be held in thraldom by anything material. The body should exist only as the means of giving the fullest expression to the spirit, and liberation implies that it casts away any possible restriction.

If there are rumblings to help to abolish bondage, slavery, thraldom, these are good because discontent over darkness, imprisonment, mental, physical or spiritual, is to be encouraged.

Love is not physical, it is spiritual. The fact of earthly parents providing a vehicle for a soul has no eternal significance. What is eternal is the attracting power of love. Love is the fulfilling of the law. And the law is the law of the Great Spirit. So the affinity exists because there is love.

You have assured me. Just occasionally I hear and read about affinity. I feel satisfied to know that this great love does still exist.

You cannot destroy love because love is eternal, love is. infinite. You cannot change that which is of the spirit and make it into nothing. Love will always endure.

You do not realise the extent to which spirit power is at work ensuring that what is best for humanity on earth and all creatures who share the planet with you should have the utmost opportunities for evolving.

The fight is not easy. Your Bible talks about the war between the powers of darkness and of light. These powers exist. Light is stronger than darkness. Light will always pierce the darkness. But there are times when the darkness is very thick and it takes longer for the light to penetrate.

So you get weary in your struggles and ask: "What are *they* doing? Why don't *they* do something?"

We are always doing something. But we have to deal with

the foolish people in your world, some of them . the worst enemies of the causes they seek to serve. The biggest obstacles are all too often people attached to movements and who stand in the way of their progress.

It has been a hard, long struggle. I know we have broken through even in the most unlikely places. We will not for one moment be deflected. Never will. we in any way turn aside from the great purpose to which we have given the whole of our lives.

I wish you were gifted with that vision that would enable you to see the plan as it is in operation. Then you would. never fear. There would never be sorrow. You would know that come what may, all will be well, divinely well. The universe is directed by the infinite power of love accompanied by wisdom. Love on its own is superb, but with the corollary of wisdom this inseparable pair will achieve all that is needed.

Keep stout hearts. Do not worry about the opposition or the foolish ones. Be sorry for them and for their missed chances. They are hurting themselves and the causes they serve. But with patience you will find they are taken out of the way.

In the battles in which we are engaged we have to be sure of our earthly generals. We do not want officers who desert their posts in crises. We want them to stand and fight and ensure that victory is won. If you are tested in the fray, make sure that you emerge stronger. That is the whole point of the test.

The, homes in which you live are blessed by the radiance of the spirit. Within their walls dwells the power of the spirit. This is the greatest power in the universe, the power of love expressing itself in your world.

What your world needs is so simple, love in action. It can transform lives and show how foolish are strife and fratricide, greed and jealousy. If only they. will share the lavish bounty of the Great Spirit all could live in happiness, harmony, concord and co-operation. It is all there for them to use rightly. Man's stupidity and cupidity are .the obstacles to be overcome.

But, like everything, love has its opposite. Of hate, Silver Birch said:

Hatred is never right. It is wrong to hate. You must love. You must even try to love those who hate you and those who would do their worst to you.

You must love in its most compassionate form. The acme of spiritual healing, for example, is compassionate love. Without compassion healing exists only in its physical or magnetic state. With compassion the spirit power is beginning to operate and there is love in action. This is the divine, the Great Spirit being reflected in the service that you render. We must try to supplant hatred with love because this is transforming darkness into light.

One visitor said this meant, to him, trying to "love the seemingly unlovable." Another commented: "This seems terribly difficult. cult. Where does one begin?" The guide replied:

There will always be the few, not many, through whom the love of the Great Spirit will shine. The real work is not done by the many but by the few. It is always the cranks, the pioneers and revolutionaries who have performed the greatest service. Work with those who are animated by .the power of love and desire to manifest it in even greater measure. The Great Spirit is not in a hurry as you are. The Great Spirit has been in charge of the universe for a very long time.

The question of hurt arose when another guest told the guide: "I have a meeting which is tremendously important and I need spiritual help. A decision has to be made." He explained that in making such a decision affecting the whole organisation, he might have to hurt one or two people, with adverse results in their everyday life. Why were we called on to

*make decisions of this nature? Did the spirit world understand
the seriousness and responsibility entailed in such crises?
Silver Birch replied:*

The good of the many is the priority and it all depends on
the motive, which is the determining factor in every action.
Confronted with any situation in which decisions have to be
made, you must be sure your motive is for the good of the whole
or the many. And you must be still to allow your conscience,
the divine monitor, to give its unerring directive.

*After the visitor detailed the nature of the problem and the
issue that involved his organisation and leading people in it,
the guide said:*

We are all part of a divine plan devised by infinite intelligence.
This plan is simple on the surface but very complex. Its
fulfilment depends on many intricacies and subtleties, the use
of delicate vibrations, the drawing together of the right people
in the right place at the right time.

In essence that plan is to ensure that the power of the spirit
shall abide in your world for all time, that no person, or collection
of people, should be able to banish it, as has happened in days
gone by. Then the outpouring of the spirit was sporadic. Now
it is here to stay in your world as its permanent possession.

And so it has infiltrated all round your globe. In practically
every country there are bridgeheads where the power of the
spirit has been consolidated to ensure it will provide what is
so essential to your world. This plan is in operation in your
land, where you and others have a responsibility to discharge,
to ensure that the power of the spirit should manifest in its
richest, greatest and most constructive measure.

There will be obstacles to overcome. The powers that be
are implacably determined that the outpouring of the spirit
is to perform its beneficent work in this land which has been
chosen to give a lead to other countries. We. require human

instruments to fulfil themselves, to. utilise their gifts without thought of self and serve wherever they can, drying the tears of mourners, mending broken hearts, healing the sick, giving strength to the weary and guidance for those who have lost their way. This is the task.

When the subject of jealousy. arose, the spirit guide told the questioner:

You must always feel sorry for those who have the knowledge and do not allow themselves to follow its implication in their daily lives. It is the greater sin against the spirit when you have the knowledge and you do not live in harmony with the law than when you are ignorant. It is sad, but there is nothing we can do about it. This is their responsibility.

The Great Spirit is very wise because the natural law ensures that you are responsible for what you do and not for what anybody else does. No matter how much you love others you cannot live their lives for them. That they must' do for themselves. The measure of your responsibility is how you acquit yourself from day to day. The law works by the immutable sequence of cause and effect. Nobody and nothing has the power to break that sequence because it is mechanical in its operation.

Those who exhibit the faults of humanity and allow their lower natures to override their higher instincts must pay the price, just as every goodness and kindness automatically means they are the better as a result. Things that are worth doing cannot be easy. If they were then they would not be worth doing.

Asked about selfishness, the guide said there was not more now than in the past. He added:

You are the victims of an era that is so cataclysmic it turns upside down many attitudes. You certainly have a tremendous materialism governing a large part of your world's inhabitants.

There is more violence; there is even to some extent more fratricide. But that is only one part of the picture. There is much unselfishness in the service rendered by many who try to help wherever they can in diverse forms of activity to their fellows.

The picture is not one of unrelieved blackness. There is light breaking through in many places. But those who have the knowledge must be optimistic because they are convinced the divine plan will be fulfilled. Man can delay, man can hinder, man can obstruct; but man cannot prevent the fulfilment of the plan.

The acquisition of knowledge brings responsibility. That responsibility is to order your life in the light of the knowledge. We are concerned with the demonstration of the spirit as a primal reality throughout your world.

All your troubles derive from the fact that ignorance of spirit truths leads people to pursue materialistic gospels; selfishness, exploitation, greed, lust for power, war, cruelty, all these are the antitheses of spiritual principles.

If you are aware of spiritual reality then you know that mercy, tolerance, compassion, service, co-operation and helping the suffering are essential. It is not enough to enjoy the beauty and richness that spiritual knowledge brings. Indeed, this can become selfish.

The purpose is not merely for one or more individuals to retain what they have learned because it illumines their lives and brings them understanding. The knowledge has to be spread and applied because your world is the place where the spirit incarnates to live in conditions that will enable it to flower.

The squalor, oppression and all the horrible actions that blacken your world cannot help in the development of the spirit of those who are at the receiving end. It is spiritually wrong to exploit your neighbour or anybody. It is wrong to inflict cruelty on others. You cannot divorce ethics and morality from spiritual principles. They are part and parcel of one and the same thing.

To say that you are religious, that you believe in God and you praise the God in song and word and regularly attend services of worship does not necessarily achieve anything spiritual. It should be the means of inspiring you to help others, so that they can e live in the light and not the darkness. All the stress from our world is directed towards helping you to perform those tasks that will make earth a better place for those who dwell in it. No, the two go together. There are no watertight compartments.

There may be some good in people living in mountain fastnesses and practising various exercises of meditation and attunement. It increases their awareness. But it is more important that people should end cruelty. Suffering there always will be. But needless suffering deliberately inflicted by man, that is not part of the divine plan.

Since some might see selfishness as, for want of a better word, sin, here are the guide's views on that human failing. Faced with the problem, "When is an earthly sin not a spiritual one and how would the spirit world describe it?" Silver Birch explained:

This depends on your codes of ethics and morality which vary from country to country in your world. What is regarded as immoral in one land is not so in another. There are sins, for example, so labelled by varying religious bodies that are not sinful. They are views and actions of people whom they consider have transgressed views which they uphold.

It all hinges on the definition of what you regard as a sin. I would say sin is that which does harm to the sinner and to others. Sin is something that demeans the person who does it and injures others. There are sins of envy, greed, jealousy, and those performing evil actions. A sin must be something that is the reverse of giving a service.

Would you agree with the definition of sin in the New Testament that sin is lawlessness, anything which breaks spiritual law?

Yes, if it is an attempt to contravene a spiritual law then it is a sin. But if it is an attempt to defy a man-made law then it is not necessarily a sin. There are people who are tied together in marriage in your world who are not spiritual partners for one another. From the standpoint of the spirit this could be a sin if they hurt one another. It all depends on how you view the problem. If you maintain spiritual standards, there is no difficulty in finding the answers.

Do you on the Other Side accept there is sin?

Oh yes, transgression of natural law is sin.

You always said you prefer the word "mistakes."

Often it is the result of ignorance rather than deliberate action. But the number of wicked people in your world is comparatively small compared with the vast population. You must be very careful not to become too condemnatory because there are very minor faults that people have. If you hate people you are sinning. I think the issue is very simple. Anything which offends your conscience is contrary to the spiritual law.

You do not first have to commit sins before you can evolve. You are imperfect physical beings in an imperfect physical world. The object of your existence is to allow the innate divinity, which is latent perfection, gradually to express itself. As it does so, the imperfections soon begin to fall away and you embark on the path of infinite progress. You do not have deliberately to plunge into the depths in order to rise. You have enough imperfections before doing that.

Sin is an action that harms the one who does it and its

receiver. More often than not, it is unconscious sinning, not deliberate, but due to ignorance, temper or haste. Instead of self-control, the individual loses his composure. He thinks, says and does things which in calmer moments of reflection he will regret.

The greatest sin is always to hurt people, not only physically, but mentally and spiritually. Always you should try to help wherever you can. If your help is rejected, then be sorry for the one who had the chance and turned it down.

A circle member interjected, "But you have said this is the earthly school where we make mistakes."

You make mistakes many times and learn from them, if you are wise enough not to repeat them. It is through making mistakes that you learn. It is from falling down that you pick yourself up. It is not the mistakes that are so terrible, because they will help you. What is bad and wrong is to deny others what you can give them, to behave unjustly and uncharitably. Do good wherever you can, that is the object of your existence.

When antagonism and injustice were mentioned, Silver Birch told his questioners:

Antagonism and hostility are the children of ignorance. They are irrational. Sometimes they are due to fear. At other times they are the result of what you call brainwashing. Minds have become polluted and are unable to reason apart from a set, predetermined course based on teaching given when they were too young to resist.

You must be sorry for them. How sad it is to see millions of people in your world living in darkness when they could be in the light. Why should so many prefer ignorance to knowledge, superstition to truth?

It is sad for them because the whole purpose of their being on earth is to have a spiritual awakening, to achieve awareness and, as a result, to have the guide lines that will enable them to live so that they do not waste their earthly years, and are ready for the next stage of their eternal existence when death comes to them as it must to all.

If you meet with antagonism, just pray for help that you may be given the words which can help those who alas have not yet found the rich jewel of truth which you possess. And if you can help them, then your meeting has not been in vain. If you cannot help them it means they are not ready. And when the soul is not ready there is nothing you can do.

I always tell my friends that what is expected is to do the best you can. You are human beings with imperfections that have to be outworked gradually until you eliminate them. But this is a long task and will not be achieved in one earthly existence.

In your world there is so much injustice and inequality. Some have too much, some have too little. Some find their path easy to travel. For others it is difficult and full of stones that make it harder. But this is the reason why you incarnate into earth so that through the variety of experiences it can offer, you can develop your spiritual nature to its greatest possible degree.

If you could see with spiritual eyes, you would realise that it is better to have an earth life with problems and hardships, with adversity and struggle, because all these are challenges to the soul and enable it to express more of its latent divinity. If you could see with spiritual eyes, you would be sorry for those who live only on the surface where all things appear materially well, with no problems to irk them.

Yet so perfect is the natural law that a balance is struck, not often in your world because it is not possible, but when the soul leaves earth and takes up its life in the world that you call Beyond. Really it is a part of one unfolding life. There are no lines of demarcation between the life in your world and in ours. Life, the essence, is spirit, not matter.

What I am trying to tell you is that you have much to make

you rejoice. The trials, tests, difficulties and problems are all part of the soul's pilgrimage. In the fullness of time it is travail that helps the soul to unfold, not lotuseating, not tasting to the full all that matter and sense have to offer. The law of compensation will, because it must, fulfil itself.

The whole purpose of earthly life is to make mistakes and learn from them, to fall and pick yourself up, to meet the daily adventure, to realise always that you are a spirit with a body, and that what is most important is the effect on the spirit, to get your priorities right and to hold on to the fundamentals.

You come to earth to enrich the soul, so that through the widest possible gamut of experiences it develops, unfolds and grows in stature and strength, and exhibits at the end of your earthly life more of the latent divinity than when you began. That is what it is all about.

Too many people, even with a little knowledge, think of themselves as bodies with spirits and their focus is all wrong. If the spirit is right, the body will be right. If the spirit fails to find the expression which is its natural manifestation, then the body will suffer.

There are two sets of complementary laws at work, those that govern matter and those that regulate the spirit. If you transgress the laws reigning over matter then there are bodily disorders, weaknesses emerge and health suffers.

But if you live your life aright, and you are in harmony with the natural laws controlling the spirit, mind and body, then you achieve not only health but the realisation that you are firmly placed on the path which is yours to tread. It will lead you into growing awareness and attainment. This is the purpose of being.

Frustrations are part of the system. You cannot exist without checks and restraints. Occasionally you can be inspired to move forward. There are other times when, for your own sake, you must be held back. But the law is perfect and always fulfils itself, ensuring that each soul receives exactly its due.

The great difficulty is you become so immersed in material things that you forget the eternal, spiritual principles on which all, life is based. When you are harassed, frustrated or impatient, because you cannot achieve what you desire,. you fail to see that the most important is what happens to the real you and not the body.

For those who have work to do there cannot be any primrose path or a bed of roses. The most beautiful roses have thorns to protect them.

So there it is, action and reaction, progress and retrogression, all part and parcel of the natural law to ensure that you move according to the stage of evolution you have reached.

But you have found, as have many others, that what has been of inestimable help is the knowledge of spiritual realities ''that you attained in the years gone by. These always provide a solid foundation, so that when the winds blow, the storms rage and the clouds obscure the sun, you know. that you receive all possible help. I wish that many more could have this knowledge.

At another circle meeting, a visitor admitted that despite "all the knowledge, the wonderful evidence and the love which surrounds us, things go wrong. I seem to slip back into depression." What could be done to avoid it? Silver Birch advised her:

Stop being depressed. There is for every soul a time when it experiences loneliness, however close others may be, but do not allow depression to secure any hold over you. With the knowledge you have there is nothing to fear in your world or in mine.

You have the evidence of being surrounded by love. This love will sustain, guard and guide you all the time. It is not always easy when you are immersed in the material problems and difficulties of earthly life. I am familiar with them. I have worked close to your world for a long time.

But I would be failing in my duty if I did not reiterate that all these are ephemeral, transient. You have within you the power that belongs to the armoury of the spirit on which you can call when physical strength seems absent. You can always withdraw into the silence of the soul and allow this inner strength to surge through your being. And it will always be accompanied by the radiance of love from our world. It requires discipline, which is always good for you. You will come through all right, as you have done. If you have any doubts, cast your mind back and see how you have been helped. Because of that, know that you will be helped whatever the morrows bring for you.

Loneliness was also discussed after the question, `Why are some people left entirely alone in this world? Silver Birch explained:

Often because they have chosen that as being necessary for their soul's evolution. But physical loneliness does not mean there is also spiritual loneliness. If awareness could be developed and latent talents expressed, then everyone who is physically lonely would be conscious of the many things surrounding them. They would know that many are bound to them by ties of love, affection, friendship or kinship.

A circle member said, "So, in effect, nobody is left entirely alone in the world."

No, the natural law is such, as you have heard me say many times, that nobody in your world is overlooked, forgotten, neglected or outside the scheme of its operation. The natural, law is comprehensive. There is no individual, no animal, no form of life that is outside the control of natural law. Everything is true to its pattern. Everything unfolds according to the law of its growth. The natural law is perfect. The natural law. fulfils itself. The natural law ensures that the will of the Great Spirit must prevail.

This led another circle member to comment on what was involved in physical and spiritual loneliness. The guide said: This is a matter for comparison. You can have a lonely person in a vast multitude. You can have spiritual loneliness because the soul is treading the path towards self-mastery and attainment which means automatically divorcing it from others. It depends how you interpret loneliness. Physical loneliness means being bereft of the companionship of others. Spiritual loneliness can be an ideal worthy of attainment.

How do you help lonely people with no knowledge of spirit truths?

You cannot help when they are not ready. This is one of the saddest of all experiences, that those who are spiritually deaf or blind cannot be helped because they are not open to. receive it. You must bide your time until the thick wall that surrounds them can begin to be penetrated by a crack, however small.

Such individuals must experience a crisis, perhaps an illness or some form of suffering which will touch the soul. This brings the beginning of an understanding that matter is not all, but only the semblance worn by reality. You cannot give anything to those who are not ready to receive it.

But none in your world is denied the opportunity of receiving truth and understanding. At some stage that opportunity will present itself. The Great Spirit has not overlooked them. They are spirit in essence even though they are unaware of that fact. As part of the plan there will come some chance so that they can become aware. It is possible they will fail. In that case it is very sad for they have missed the purpose of earthly life.

A circle member pointed oat that as people get very old they were more likely to lose earthly relatives and friends. How were they to blame for being lonely? The guide insisted:

You cannot judge purely by the material aspect because you are unaware of the spiritual considerations involved. What is best for them still may be to endure that loneliness because it is the only way they can learn the lesson for which they incarnated into earth.

Frequently, Silver Birch has been asked about problems and difficulties. None of us can escape them. But here the guide puts life's trials and tribulations into perspective. His composite comments are taken from various circles.

Sometimes in earthly life you have to dwell in the shadows. When that happens remember it is part, not the whole. The shadow exists because it is cast by the light of the sun which is there even when you cannot see it.

Shadows are ephemeral. They do not last. In due course they dissolve and fade and allow the light to illumine your being. Hold on to all the knowledge that has been given to you, to the foundation on which you can always build and face the problems that inevitably arise in your world.

It is not possible to have an earthly existence freed from problems, difficulties or troubles because that is why you are born into your world. What is important is the way you face them and call on the indwelling, latent divinity to provide the strength to find the solutions and draw you to do what is right.

When you make a link with our world it cannot be broken. It opens a channel through which the power of the spirit reaches you. And in that form of transmission there is all that is necessary for the well-being of your spirit, mind and body.

You all know it, but you do not practise it. You allow yourselves to become bogged down by the problems of your world which require attention, by the cares that beset you, and give them a magnified existence that is not real. Everything physical is only the pale reflection, the shadow of the spiritual reality.

Matter of itself has no existence. Matter exists because it is activated by the spirit. Spirit is life and the power you receive is exactly the same as the life force. You are partakers in the process of creation. If you live aright, and think aright, you can share in all the infinite bounty that the spirit has to offer.

By ordering your lives in harmony with this knowledge you automatically have at your disposal everything that is essential for your well-being, spiritually, mentally and physically. It is the thought that is wrong in allowing the physical things to predominate too much.

I am not suggesting you should disregard your obligations to the world in which you live, or to the physical body through which you express yourself. But if your thought is right, and you achieve the harmony and concord as a result, then all you require must come to you.

That is why you are on earth, so that you can triumph over all that is negative and be spiritually stronger as a result. I am not saying this is easy. It is difficult. But the attainment of spiritual values cannot be easy because it involves a rigorous mental training so that your perspective and focus are always correct.

There are times when purely physical weaknesses militate against your achieving the right balance. But you can conquer them by calling on the inner power that is yours. There is nothing stronger than the divinity within your spiritual armoury that has all the weapons to fight against anything that is negative.

This is what we try to teach and instil into, your minds, so that your attitude to all that life brings you is the right one, and that spiritually you are the better for whatever you have to encounter. There will always be problems while you are on earth, because your world is where you learn your lessons. And to learn them they sometimes have to contain difficulties for you to master.

But you should have the confidence, born of knowledge, that all life is spirit, that the power of life is not in the seen but in the unseen. You are surrounded by tremendous love in our world, not only from your own, but from others who strive to help as much as they can.

Welcome the challenges that earth has to offer. I can say without fear of contradiction that I know of no case where those who have served have been forgotten and lack the necessities of earthly life.

It is not when life is rosy that the soul grows. It is only when facing the challenge that it has the opportunity to exhibit its latent divinity and strength, so that these can. rise to the surface and help you to grow in mental stature and in spiritual grace. And that is ' the important thing which matters in your life.

If the whole of your earthly existence was one long monotone where all was easy, then you would accomplish nothing. Your souls would be stunted for lack of expression and unable to grow. Nature does not favour inertia. You cannot do nothing and evolve.

When you experience problems, troubles, crises, difficulties and hardships, as inevitably you must, pause, reflect, and let the power of the spirit show the way and give you the chance to turn them to your spiritual advantage.

You might say it is very easy for me to preach this gospel because I do not have to experience these conditions. But I am very familiar with them, not only having experienced them on earth, but also by virtue of the fact that I have to work closely with those I love and know what they must undergo. So keep a stout heart and maintain your usual, confident, radiant cheerfulness.

We are aware of prevailing circumstances. If you do not worry us and make the path more difficult by thoughts of fear and agitation, then it is easier for us to come to you. Grief is bad for you and for the one who has left you and come to our world. Worry is bad for you. It blocks the channel by which help can come.

The soul who knows should be calm, sure, certain that at the right time the way will be shown. You are never left alone. Sometimes it is necessary as part of your spiritual development that you must face a situation where you have to make a choice. Then we stand back to see whether you will turn to the left or the right, or go straight on. We can tell by what you do whether like good children you have learned your lessons, or like bad children you have not done so.

But it is only in the darkness that you find light. It is only in sorrow that you can find joy. It is only when all seems lost that you can find the way. It is only when the world of matter has nothing to offer that the power of the spirit can step in and show there is a rich bounty awaiting you.

As low materially as it seems sometimes people can sink, so correspondingly high can they as spiritual beings rise, so that there is ample compensation for all the experiences they have undergone. Were it not for the dark days -this is a euphemism because they were weeks, months and years-you would not have become aware of the gifts of the spirit which you have utilised to serve others and help them as you have been helped.

You can look back and see where the signpost of the spirit has pointed the way for you and brought you into a haven where there is peace within and an understanding so that you are aware of what you have still to achieve.

I cannot tell you that earthly life is very easy for you because that would not be true. But difficulties are challenges to unfolding souls. As you meet them with the resolution born of knowledge you conquer them and increase in stature as a result. You have nothing to fear as to what the morrow will bring. At any time you can look back to the past, not to dwell on its too often unhappy associations, but just to see how you have been guided when it seemed no such direction was possible.

We are all blessed because we have had the benediction of the spirit. The influx of this power into our lives is the greatest blessing that any can have. I can only urge you to go forward, to greet each new morning as the opportunity for serving and equipping your true self with the armoury it requires to do the battle of earthly living.

Leave the easy road for those who have no spiritual attainment in front of them. The hard road is for those who seek spiritual mastery and all the riches that accompany it. The prizes of the spirit` are not for those who seek easy pathways. Were they so, the prizes would not be worth having.

It is better to fight a battle and to win than not to be engaged in any combat. It is only in the struggle that the soul comes into its own and its many latent qualities have the opportunity of expressing some of their innate divinity.

Natural law is an immutable sequence of cause and effect. There are no chances, no coincidences. The question of unfairness can never arise. The Great Spirit is perfect love and perfect wisdom. Justice is always ultimately meted out so that none escapes the divine ordinances. . Whatever circumstance comes to you is challenge. The soul possesses, because of its divine origin, power and energy to meet the challenge, to overcome it and to emerge stronger as a result. You should always welcome the challenge of circumstance and refuse to be pessimistic or to complain. With the knowledge you possess you can face every day with inner exaltation because there is nothing that can harm your eternal soul.

The greatest souls have to endure the hardest earthly

existence. Greatness of soul cannot be achieved without being tested and purified, without the true mettle of the spirit being able to be shown in all its beauty, radiance and splendour. Difficulties are good for the soul and sometimes also for the body. They constitute the challenge to call on latent strength to come to the surface. Thus the individual grows, develops, unfolds and the divinity becomes more manifest.

It is the law of compensation and retribution. The law of polarity is at work. There is always redress for whatever happens in your world, just as automatically there is always the advance for anything you have achieved spiritually.

Earth life is a school where you come to learn your lessons. If they are easy you are not educated. So you must have difficulties. Only in mastering difficulties do you become truly educated in mind and spirit. If you fail to conquer hardship you have lost an opportunity for spiritual development. There is no circumstance, no hardship, no obstacle so strong that you do not possess the inner power to surmount it. Whether you call it into being is entirely for you.

One of the objects of hardship, difficulty, ill-health, bereavement and suffering is to awaken the soul to its possibilities and to allow it to begin to unfold. If earthly life were easy and everyone were materially rich and had no problems, then spiritually you would be puny weaklings. The balance must be struck. It is never part of our teaching to neglect the duties and requirements of your physical bodies. But it is equally true that you must tend your spirit as well. Both are necessary on earth.

Alas for those who cannot distinguish between the material and the spiritual. You can struggle, have difficulties and battle, but you can still have tranquillity and peace. You can face all the battles of your world and still have inner peace because you know they cannot touch you. Peace does not come from without but from within. If people in your world would only realise the armoury of the spirit with which they are equipped. They could use all this tremendous power within to help them learn to retire and cultivate the fruits of the spirit which bring tranquillity, poise, calmness and peace.

Of the great souls who live in your world, and achieve most for it with their reforms and pioneering, many have inner peace though the battle be strong and the opposition difficult. Do not equate physical happenings with spiritual principles. Spirit is master and matter is servant. Let the spirit show its mastery.

Asked if he agreed that "sometimes we have to be cruel to be kind," Silver Birch said:

The answer is very simple. It is the motive which counts. If your motive is a desire to serve, that will qualify the action you perform. The Great Spirit has so ordered it that every one of His children contains within his being the divine monitor of conscience which automatically announces that what you are doing, saying or thinking is right or wrong. In reality you always have the answer as to what to do. There is no cheating. The law will always operate. Physically you can pretend, spiritually you cannot. Physically you are a closed book, spiritually you are an open page. This is the great difference.

Progress is achieved because you have earned it. There are no instant methods of achieving spiritual mastery. Every step must be taken successively. You become what you have made yourself to be by the way you live. No one can deflect or. change in any way that immutable sequence of cause and effect in your lives. That is how the law works. Thus does the Great Spirit ensure that justice always will be done, not necessarily in your world of matter, but it will operate when you come to our side of life.

The next two-part question was: "Is there any point at

which apparent cruelty no longer matters? Would any purpose be served by, say, taking a snail from a thrush?"

There is no point where cruelty has a purpose to serve, where those responsible for perpetrating it are concerned. When you come to the animal kingdom you are confronted with the operation of different laws which, though they are part of the same whole, operate in a fashion that is designed to allow nature to fulfil itself.

The snail and the thrush are part of nature which, left to its own devices, will ensure that the balance is always struck. If you consider that you should remove the snail then do so. But it does not lie within your province to remove all the snails from all the thrushes. What cannot be excused, and carries within itself the seeds of its own punishment, is the needless cruelty perpetrated by humans on one another and on animals.

The question and answer session continued. "There are thousands, perhaps millions, of people suffering in the world today. Are they all souls paying for past misdeeds? Have they had to come back to suffer?"

They are part and parcel of the one great evolutionary ladder. It is not possible to give a simple answer to cover a complex law at work. To judge physical, happenings without the knowledge of spiritual qualification must fail. Rest your faith-because this is a matter of faith, not knowledge-on what has been revealed to you, that the Great Spirit is the epitome of love and wisdom, and justice is done to all in time.

Your world is only one little aspect of being. It is not the whole of eternity. There is compensation and there is retribution. Every soul does come into its own. If you attempt to judge the Great Spirit by the infinitesimal fraction that you see operating in your physical world, you will fail because you are obviously unaware of all the other aspects that form part of eternity.

Nothing is ever forgotten, nothing is overlooked,. nothing is neglected. The law encompasses all. Every being, every aspect, every facet, small or large, simple or complex, all are part of the immutable law. Where you cannot understand, realise that you are dealing with something you cannot measure. You are limited perforce by the restriction that the physical body imposes on your soul. But love reigns supreme. The Great Spirit is love and love fulfils itself in time with all.

We come back to your world because we love you. We will do everything in our power to help you, but we cannot give you what you are not able to assimilate. It is only through growth that understanding comes. Each rung on the ladder reveals, as you climb it, the rung above, and all these rungs stretch towards infinity. I cannot solve all your problems for you because there are factors that cannot be made clear to you.

The knowledge you have received must be the base on which to build your faith, not unreasoning, incredulous faith, but the faith which is founded on what has been shown to you, that there is a divine plan ordained by divine love and wisdom, and at all times you are encompassed by it. This should make you realise that whatever happens to you or anybody else in your world is part of the plan.

There is no difficulty so great that you have not the power within and without to help you to overcome it and emerge as a result greater in spiritual stature. This is the whole object of your earthly existence, to learn your lessons and to be the better equipped spiritually as a result.

If at any time doubts come into your mind, then pause. Let your minds go back to the days that are past and realise how you have been led to bring you where you are today. You are fortunate to be in possession of these wondrous truths that have continued to illuminate your earthly lives. They have brought you the great link with your own loved ones and others not of your kith and kin but spiritually related to you. Their desire is to co-operate so that together we can help so many others who, alas, live in a miasma of ignorance. This is the reason for our returning to you.

Chapter Eight

ORTHODOXY EXAMINED AND INDICTED

TODAY, if the Nazarene were to return to your world and listen to the doctrines taught in his name, he would not recognise them. Many of them are not what he taught; they are the inventions of priests.

These were among the comments Silver Birch made to an Anglican clergyman paying his first visit to the circle. The priest put his problem to the guide: "I find your teaching very helpful. I am a minister, but I get very depressed with dogmas and organised religion. Yet I find some goodness in the Church. I am perplexed whether to work from within or from without."

Let us begin at the beginning. Your church, like every other church, temple, synagogue and chapel, owes its existence to the fact that in days gone by the power of the spirit descended in your world. It was accompanied by what are called signs and wonders and sometimes miracles.

The power of the spirit came as a challenge to the beliefs, the doctrines, the dogmas of that day. The power of the spirit gave evidence of its divine origin in that its beneficence was demonstrated in healing the sick, in giving guidance and in stressing the fundamental principles of life that matter is a shell and spirit the reality. But alas, the pages of your history show that all such outpourings lasted for only a short while.

Gradually the theologians took control and the mind of man devised teachings which replaced revelations that were divine. Sterility superseded revelation. Again and again there have been some outpourings of the spirit accompanied by signs and wonders and what were believed miracles. And the process was constantly repeated.'

These kind of churches were described graphically by the Nazarene as whited sepulchres, because the power of the spirit has been driven out from them. Orthodoxy has built such a formidable wall it makes it impossible for that sublime power to break through. That is the indictment which in all candour I must make.

The problem arises when men like yourself become aware of the truths of the spirit which in many cases contradict their creedal beliefs. So what does one do in such circumstances? I say stay where you are and enlighten those who will listen to you. You need not use words like "Spiritualism." It is only a label. We are not concerned with labels. We are concerned with liberating souls, giving them the enfranchisement that will enable them to live as the Great Spirit intended.

The troubles of your world are largely due to the fact that materialism dominates the actions and thoughts of millions of people. Greed and avarice are the malignant cancers that infect your plane. These have to be driven out by knowledge, by understanding, by a realisation of the fundamental truth that all life is founded on spirit and not on matter.

This is what you can teach. You can reach people who come to you for guidance. Because of what you are you should be in a position to help them to find themselves. In the end every human being has to indulge in a process of self-regeneration. Nobody else can save him. He can only save himself. You will find that the door continually opens for you to help others.

If you leave your church you have access only to the same body of people that others who are gifted mediums and exponents have. Therefore you are only one more to add to those already performing this service. But as an ordained minister, charged with a mission, you can help those who come to you. because they consider you are a spiritual mentor for them.

The Nazarene is the guiding intelligence behind all the work we try to do. Moreover we have as helpers many like yourself who wore the cloth. Because of their added knowledge and power they seek instruments through whom they can serve others. The desire to serve does not end with physical death.

The Great Spirit, with divine wisdom, has given you a questioning mind. It will grow and develop as you use it. Honest criticism can never be offensive. We welcome those who question us because they really want to know. For .others whose one desire is to have wordy debates, challenges in semantics, this has no appeal to us. We want to serve wherever we can. When we find those whose souls have been touched because the catalyst of grief, sorrow, or difficulty has come upon them, then we can help. They are ready to receive.

The clergyman was accompanied by his wife and a woman who teaches religious instruction at a large comprehensive school. She told the guide: "I have been reading your teachings that have been recorded. In one place you have said there is no personal God apart from the one human beings have created. You say, `The Great Spirit is the Law.' Also you have said: `Through all eternity there is the love of God and the God of love. And each time you express that love you help God to express himself.' From this and other teachings I gain the impression that you are speaking in personal terms of God. Would you clarify this, please?"

I will try, but it is very, very difficult because to attempt a definition of the infinite in finite language-is virtually impossible. The Great Spirit is not a person in the sense that you understand personality. The Great Spirit is not a magnified human being. The Great Spirit is not a man or a woman.

The Great Spirit is the supreme power, infinite intelligence, love, compassion, wisdom, the epitome of all spiritual qualities and principles. But to convey some idea of the Great Spirit we are forced to use your language. If I refer to the Great Spirit as "It" this would cause more difficulties than if I say "Him."

Your universe, like others, is ruled by immutable, natural laws. These have always been in existence; these will always be in existence. They do not have to be changed because of unforeseen circumstances arising. They do not have to be repealed because new conditions have. arisen over which they have no control. They are perfect in their operations, requiring neither suspension nor abrogation, because they were devised by infinite intelligence.

Wherever there is life the natural law operates. Effect always follows cause; reaping always follows sowing. None has the power to intervene between cause and effect, or to change what must be an unalterable sequence. Wherever new discoveries are made-in your world, it is found that they operate under law. There is no chance, no coincidence; the natural laws comprise all and everything.

Is not this fact an indication of the sublime intelligence that created the laws and ensures that they sustain every facet of manifestation of being and activity? And is it not also evidence that love rules throughout all these natural laws and that perfect justice must prevail?. Goodness brings its own reward just as sin brings its own punishment.

The last rites given by a priest will not change the operation of natural law. The prayer offered, however sincere, cannot change the operation of natural law. Acceptance of any creed cannot change the operation of natural law, for it must operate in order to ensure that perfect justice prevails. None can remove the results of your actions from your shoulders. You are personally responsible for everything you do and think.

The saint and the sinner do not share an equality of spiritual stature. And none can cheat or pretend. This is the Great Spirit and what the Great Spirit means.

When you speak of personality, the Great Spirit is personal in the sense that the Great Spirit is within every individual. And the Great Spirit is impersonal in the sense that the Great Spirit is the law. So the Great Spirit is not a vengeful deity with partiality for some and punishment for others. The law operates to ensure that effect will follow cause. The Great Spirit is within you. That seed of divinity is implanted from the moment of conception. You have the opportunity in your daily life to allow it to flower, to bloom and to manifest its hidden richness.

Would it be true to say that all comes within the compass of the Great Spirit?

Yes, the Great Spirit is everywhere. You cannot be where the Great Spirit is not.

In the New Testament the Nazarene said you cannot put new wine into old bottles. How does that link up with what you have been saying?

You cannot put new wine into old bottles. What you can do is to put old wine into new bottles. You cannot compel the power of the spirit so that it can be fitted into predetermined beliefs. You cannot make spirit truths fit your pattern of belief. You must reject at any time any belief, any doctrine, any form of words, however ancient, that you know are untrue.

The Nazarene spoke in parables, but the meaning is quite clear. If you are aware of spirit power, if you are cognisant of spirit truths, then you cannot - expound any doctrine which is contradictory to them. It is as simple as that. I was asked about the Great Spirit. The Great Spirit is not three in one as it is said somewhere. The Great Spirit is everything, everywhere. The Great Spirit comprises all universal life. If you believe that the

Great Spirit can be separated into three parts of a trinity, then what you believe is wrong. Besides, what does it matter? Does it help you spiritually to believe the Great Spirit is three in one?

The original questioner said, "I found it very confusing."

So do I. Give your allegiance to the truth as revealed to you. To believe in the unbelievable is no credit to your intelligence. Neither will it help your soul to grow.

When a "dissatisfied clergyman in the Church of England" visited the circle for "an evening my wife and I will never forget," the guide greeted him by saying:

I know you are familiar with some of the truths I have tried to teach. In your own way, after much heart-searching and inner tribulation, you have turned your back on the creeds and doctrines of the past and have grasped the truths of the spirit which have illumined your life for you.

I wish that others who have been in your position were as accessible to the power of the spirit and to its sublime truths as you have been. It is a piteous spectacle to contemplate that those who should be the custodians of this divine power and the ambassadors and emissaries of the Great Spirit present a stone wall that neither the power of the spirit nor its truths can penetrate.

And so their churches are cold, barren, lifeless and sterile, because the vivifying power of the spirit cannot be manifested there. So rejoice that the way was shown to you, even through sorrow, and you have found the light which has guided you and which will continue to shed its refulgent beams and illumine your pathway.

Invited to ask questions, the visitor said: "We know the Great Spirit uses you and others in the higher realms and comes through to us in that way. In the whole of history has the Great Spirit ever spoken without coming through a spirit entity?" Silver Birch replied:

The Great Spirit is not a person. The Great Spirit is not a deified individual. The Great Spirit is beyond personality. The Great Spirit is the epitome of law, love, wisdom, truth. The Great Spirit is the law, the infinite intelligence operating ceaselessly in a mighty universe.

The Great Spirit is to be seen in the countless manifestations of natural phenomena. The Great Spirit is to be witnessed in the demonstrations of love when His children perform deeds of heroism, self-abnegation, mercy and serve those less fortunate than themselves. The Great Spirit is visible in the flow of that power which heals the sick, comforts the mourner, uplifts the fallen. The Great Spirit cannot manifest as a man or a woman. But some of the essence of the Great Spirit which is within every one of His children can be expressed.

Can we speak direct to the Great Spirit? If so, is it the Great Spirit within ourselves?

You are the Great Spirit, the Great Spirit is you. The difference is not in kind or in essence but in degree. The Great Spirit is the acme of perfection, for which you will infinitely strive. So the Great Spirit is within and without. When you express qualities of divinity, love, tolerance, mercy, compassion, charity, you are communicating with the Great Spirit because the Great Spirit is being communicated through you.

Now the Great Spirit has many messengers, many channels. The Great Spirit has a hierarchy of beings whose purpose is to ensure that the divine will is made manifest. So you can, if you like, talk to the Great Spirit in silence, by meditation, verbally by prayer, which often is a good thing because it helps to crystallise the thought which may wander and meander and give it a concreteness of expression which otherwise it would not have.

But whether silent or spoken, the true yearning of every soul is known to the Great Spirit and to alll those who are charged with the task of administering the laws of the Great Spirit.

Have you ever met the Nazarene in the spirit world?

Yes I have, many times. I have told my friends here about it. Always when I withdraw from your world, which I do regularly, to attend the gathering where the Nazarene is always present. He is concerned with spreading these truths, of which he was an exemplar on earth, long since buried by those who claim to follow him.

These are being resurrected, accompanied by the demonstration of the same power of the spirit which operated in his day. Nothing causes greater sorrow to the Nazarene and to all the hierarchy than to see the way in which those who are ecclesiastical superiors are so abysmally ignorant of simple spiritual truths.

So you have found the light. Rejoice that you have done so and know that the same power which guided you and provided the unerring signposts will continue to point the way. It has not been easy. But the easy way is not for those who have work to do.

If these could not surmount the troubles that befall them, they cannot rank as officers in the great war being waged by the world of spirit against the parasitical materialism of your world.

Thank the Great Spirit for the truth that has brought so muchwarmth and love into your hearts, for the love which you thought you had lost and found and which has brought you where you are now. Rejoice. You have in your possession a treasure which, in the words of the Bible, moth and rust cannot touch. It will be undimmed, translucent, radiant and yours for all time because you have earned it.

It is also apposite to quote what the guide told two American clerical visitors – one was a canon – on their visit. Silver Birch, as always, gave the guests a warm welcome:

You are doing a very good work. This is not easy, but it is very necessary where you live that the light of the spirit shall drive out the prevailing darkness and substitute the worship of truth for that of the golden calf.

It is important because there are millions of souls in despair who know not where to turn. I know you will forgive me when I say it is unfortunate there are not hundreds, thousands perhaps, of the clergy who are able to help them in their crisis and point the way that will bring them spiritual, mental and physical freedom.

This is the task on which you are engaged. It is sad that the churches, which are built for the one purpose of revealing divine truths, have become places where the power of the spirit cannot operate because of barriers that man has built.

And it is sad that clergymen, who should be the spiritual leaders, teachers.and masters, are bereft of spiritual truth and, even worse, prefer man-made creeds to divine inspiration which is available today. Please do not think I say this as harsh strictures. I am enunciating only that which is a very regrettable fact.

But the light is breaking through and the power of the spirit is here to stay in your world. It will continue to stream through in an ever-increasing number of human channels. It will demonstrate that the Great Spirit is not without witnesses even in your own time and that every child of the Great Spirit has access to the divine fount.

It will reveal that sublime power and beneficence are available if the children of the Great Spirit will order their lives so that they are capable of receiving them. They will come to you because through difficulty, heartbreak, bereavement and sickness they will be spiritually ready to have their souls touched.

Do not waste your time on those who merely wish to have

theological debates about the interpretation of doctrine or dogma. This has no value and will not increase any person's spirituality by one jot. It does not matter because it is arid and pointless. Wait for those who are ready. Be available. Offer truth wherever you can. If it is rejected, feel sorry for those who have had the chance and do not take it.

The natural law is so perfect that every child of the Great Spirit while on earth has one opportunity of finding himself. He can have his soul touched, so that the divine spark can be kindled and fanned into a beauteous flame and some of the richness, dignity, beauty, splendour, nobility and grandeur of the latent divine spirit brought into expression. This opportunity comes to all. If you can help one to find the way then it is all worth while.

There are mighty hosts of the spirit, evolved, liberated beings, part of the hierarchy, who are deeply concerned with worldly conditions, with the maelstrom, chaos, violence, destruction, greed, cupidity and jealousy, all products of a materialism that grows on the human body politic.

These must be uprooted, so that man can come into his own and have an awareness of what he is, why he is in your world and what- he can achieve to transform it into a kingdom of heaven. This is what your world is intended to be when all live according to the light of the spirit.

You have the inestimable privilege of serving in this mighty cause. You have been guided. However difficult it may be, however irksome, remember you are never alone. The light of the spirit is with you and the love of the spirit encompasses you wherever you may be.

I have said it many times, to serve is noble. There can be no higher service than that which is done for the Great Spirit to His children. And there is no higher or greater religion than that of service.

Religion which is merely formal and gives subservience to doctrine has no value. Religion is that which enables and compels people to go out into the world and make it better because of what they do.

When things become difficult, when storm clouds gather, lightning flashes and thunder roars, be still and know that the power which has guided you will continue in its own way to show what is the next step for you.

Go forward. Do the best you can. No more is expected of you. When you fall down pick yourself up. That is why you fall down. You will make mistakes because you are imperfect beings in an imperfect world and the pilgrimage towards perfection is eternal. So be grateful for all that has been made manifest to you.

At other circle meetings came these penetrating comments: What you are trying to do is to touch souls. I have told many of my friends in your world who do the healing, which is among the greatest gifts of all, that when the body is healed, it is excellent. But if the body is healed and the soul is not touched, then the healing has failed from our point of view.

It is touching souls that matters. It is making every individual in your world aware of the fact that he is a spark of the divine. And it is your service to kindle that spark, to fan it, so that the individual becomes aware of his innate divinity, and what was a spark becomes a glowing, lambent flame.

That is what you call in your world the object of the exercise. Evidence for survival after physical death is very important. But it is not designed only to assuage grief, vital though that might be. It is designed, like the healing, to bring awareness of spiritual realities.

I said this is a unique service you are performing. It should be done by the churches; the healing should be done by your doctors. But it is very sad that in the case of the churches they are, alas, blind leaders of the blind. The open vision has gone. They no longer are able to see what is around them. They have lost the ability to enjoy the richness of spirit and spiritual communication and communion. What they have to offer are merely husks, and in many cases doctrines which privately many of them no longer believe.

As for your medical men, it is sad that they are so immersed in their conventional treatments that in the main they oppose any other form of healing which can bring relief, betterment and cure to the growing number of sick people in your world. But even there, progress is being made.

The power of the spirit is here to stay in your world. Every centre, every group, every individual who is aware of these truths and has become a repository for them, spreading them wherever they can, is a lighthouse of the spirit. Its rays will enable pilgrims who have lost their way to find the truth that has brought you spiritual and mental freedom.

Each little lighthouse becomes a bridgehead that is consolidated and has then to be extended for another bridgehead. Thus, gradually, the power of the spirit will girdle your globe. There will be available numbers of instruments to act as the dispensers of its beauty, its glory, its radiance and its grandeur. No individual, no combination of individuals, no parliaments, no churches, no bodies of doctors or scientists, none will be able to banish the power of the spirit.

That is the task on which you are engaged. Behind it is the supreme power which cannot fail you. This is the measure of the inspiration that awaits each one of you. There is work to be done. There are many to be helped.

It is a sad commentary that despite the large number of churches, chapels, temples and reverends of many kinds they are unable to meet the spiritual aspirations of people in their own lands. Unfortunately some of them have little faith in what they proclaim as the fundamentals of religion. When they are confronted with the acid tests of bereavement, sickness, suffering and crisis they find that their ship is rudderless and cannot steer them into peaceful waters.

It is a very dark world, a very troubled world, a very violent world, a very sick world, a very distressed world. There are millions of despairing individuals who do not know, where to turn. They have lost faith in the old religions and philosophies because they feel these have let them down and cannot answer all the questions they have to ask.

Where is the religion that can explain to them who and what they are, why they are placed on earth and what happens when they come to our world? Healing plays its great part in answering these questions. When it is successful the intelligent individual must realise that the power responsible does not come from any source in your world, but from a much higher sphere of activity.

The trouble with the people in your world is that they worship mammon. Their ambitions are centred on things material. They allow themselves to be ruled by greed, selfishness and avarice, with the result that their focus is all wrong.

It is the spirit that must be seen to dominate matter and not matter that must dominate the spirit. It is the spirit that must be king and matter the subject. When the spirit rules and governs and directs, then all falls into line. Not only is health achieved, but an inner awareness, a serenity and tranquillity inevitably follow.

The violence in your world is the direct result of the sickness of the people who live in it. The change must come from within. Governments can pass laws to alter certain material conditions, but these are only temporary expedients that cannot deal with root causes, the effects of a worship of the golden calf. It is good to heal physical bodies. It is better to touch the soul so that awareness is achieved.

We are working according to a plan. We are not evangelists conducting mass meetings and capturing people in the heat of emotionalism. We labour to ensure that individuals become convinced, one at a time, that they are satisfied with the evidence they have received that they will continue after physical death, and they are also satisfied that what we have to teach neither insults their intelligence nor makes their reason revolt. We must win you by evidence, by reason, by intelligence, by affection and by co-operation.

We will not presume to dictate or to compel, but teach you to use your divine gifts to serve others, as people with divine gifts have served you. So it must be one at a time. Each individual who becomes convinced creates a magnetic link with our world which cannot be broken, and is the means by which a constant stream of power will come to him or to her.

We will continue to make progress as all these bridgeheads are gradually consolidated. The plan of the spirit will be fulfilled. We rejoice as every time another soul in your world emerges from the darkness of superstition into the light of spiritual knowledge.

There are many clergymen who have their doubts, but are afraid to express them. Many are honest, but in positions from which they cannot extricate themselves. Let us be sorry for those who should be able to lead, but instead of being in the vanguard are in the rearguard. It is the greatest condemnation of what you call Orthodoxy that you have a world in travail and it has nothing to offer because it turned its back on the light many centuries ago. We are privileged to be ambassadors of the divine. Thus it is a responsibility for us all.

It is part of the plan that the power of the spirit is being made manifest, not through archbishops, bishops, popes, priests and rabbis, but through ordinary mortals who are charged with the wonderful opportunity of helping the Great Spirit so that divine love, wisdom and power should be available to all who are ready to receive it.

If you remove tears of sorrow from one mourner; if you heal one sick person who has heard the dread verdict that he or she cannot be cured; if you have enabled one soul to find itself; if you have given direction to someone who believed he or she was in a morass or a maze from which there was no escape; then the whole of your earthly life will have been worth while.

Our task, like yours, is to enable the power of the spirit to become available to those who are ready to receive it. They will come to you in their sorrow, in their despair, in their sickness, in their perplexity, in their bewilderment, because nowhere else, in religion, in science or in philosophy, can they find what you have to offer.

It should be the labour of those who belong to the varying religions who, if they were truly qualified, would be following the injunction of the one they regard as their leader, to heal the sick and comfort the bereaved. But, alas, there are very few within the religious sphere who are able to perform any of these important tasks.

The power of the spirit is mightier than the princes of the churches. We must be sorry for them. How sad it is to see that those in positions of high office have lost their way and are incapable of having access to the same source of inspiration responsible for the religions in which they are the leaders.

A circle member asked whether any religious leaders who discovered these spirit truths should renounce their old orthodox outlook. The guide said:

We have enshrined personal responsibility as one of the supreme principles. Each soul is responsible for what it does. You cannot equivocate with the truths of the spirit. As awareness comes so the voice of conscience says what should be done. If it is accepted and recognised then that soul must do what it implies. I will not condemn individuals because it is not right and proper for me to do so.

I think it would be wrong to criticise, but should one encourage them ?

What you should do is to offer truth wherever you can. Individuals cross your path for that reason, so that you can help them just as you were helped when you needed it. This is the law and how it works, but after that your responsibility ends. All souls in your world are at differing stages of evolution and growth. There is no one single truth that will appeal to everybody.

In matters of the spirit mass conversion is not possible. The wind bloweth where it listeth. The spirit infiltrates where it can. It is the leaven constantly at work. Each individual must resolve for himself or herself as far as is possible, according to the stage of growth, attainment and progress, what the truth implies and go on from there.

What is important is for truth to effect its lodgement with that self. As I said before, when the magnetic link is made it cannot be broken. That is the means of creating the channel or the path through which or along which the power of the spirit is able to manifest.

If you act according to the truth as you see it-and neither you nor I has arrived at its finality-that is all you can do. No more and no less can be expected of you. As I have said many times, you do the best you can. You cannot do any more and you should not do any less. Every effort you make to help to spread truth, to cause error, superstition and ignorance to vanish has our blessing and our help. That is why we have returned to work in your world.

I find it very sad that those who should have the greatest knowledge of spiritual matters are the most profoundly ignorant of them. I think it a reflection on the orthodox and conventional religions of your world that they have become so atrophied and wandered so far away from the original source of their inspiration that it is indeed almost impossible to find any resemblance between the origin and its successor.

One of the primary reasons that beings like myself were asked to return and proclaim our teaching, philosophy, and ethics and enunciate the true spiritual principles on which religion should be based, is.because your many religions had failed in their task and were unable to guide those who looked to them for direction.

It is paradoxical that the power of the spirit was originally responsible for the foundation of these religions which have erected edifices in which it is conspicuously absent. Moreover, those who are leaders are not receptive to the power of the spirit, are spiritually deaf, dumb and blind, admirable people though they may be in other, respects. In their ignorance they oppose the descent of the Holy Spirit today, that same power which enabled their religion to make its mark in times gone by.

You are privileged to be the custodians and disseminators of this tremendous power of the spirit. You are making a very important contribution to your world which has been, and still is, in peril through the ignorance and blindness of those who govern its affairs. The work that you and many others do is to ensure that the power of the spirit, having established itself, will continue to broaden its influence. Thus more and more people can be made aware of who they are, what they are, why they are on earth and what it is . they must do so that they fulfil the purpose of their being.

It is pathetic to realise that there are millions, like moles burrowing in the dark, who have no understanding of life, its dynamic, its purpose and how they should order their existence so as to derive from it all the exhilaration, mental, spiritual and physical, that could be theirs.

A visitor told Silver Birch: "My scientific life has created problems that have worried me. The first is to do with the concept of God, which since I have been acquainted with Spiritualism, I find you call the Great White Spirit. Before this I developed my concept of God because I could _ not agree with the orthodox version. I decided that God could be equated only with the overall laws of nature in the widest sense, but not an entity as supposed in orthodox religion. Is this a realistic view?" The guide replied:

Let us begin with the orthodox conception which is far short of the reality. There is the immediate problem that language, being finite, cannot express the infinite. God, or the Deity, or the Great Spirit, as I prefer, is infinite, without beginning, without end, always has been, always will be. Spirit, the life force, similarly is eternal, without beginning and without end. So God, life, spirit, these have always existed. They were not the product of some spontaneous generation.

You can only picture the sublime power behind the universe in very restricted form because it is impossible to comprehend the whole. You said that you equated God with the laws of nature. But God is more than the laws of nature because God is responsible for the laws of nature. It is infinite intelligence which devised the natural laws and also the means by which they operate.

Unfortunately, for most individuals on earth, their concept of God must of necessity be anthropomorphic. They cannot visualise any being having existence except in individual form. But God is not individual in the sense that you are individuals. God is not a person in the sense that you are persons.

God is impersonal, but at the same time expresses all personality, which is difficult for you to understand. God is in all life. As life becomes individuated in human beings God is expressed in individuality as well as in the operation of the natural forces that are part of the universe, which in turn is part of the cosmos.

You have to try and visualise not a being, but Being, infinite in intelligence, wisdom, knowledge, truth, in fact, the epitome of all the divine qualities with which we are familiar. And this is God, not male, not female, but male arid female, beyond personality but immanent in all personality.

God is within all and without all. None can exist apart from God; none can be cut off from God. God is in you as God is in the rain, the sun, flowers, vegetables, in animals in all that has any aspect of existence however small it may seem to be. We are in difficulties when we try and present this picture of the Great Spirit, as I call it, the supreme power of love that directs everything, is not divorced from them, but within every manifestation of being that there is.

Another guest wanted to know: "If God is a universal spirit power of wisdom, intelligence and love in perfection, directing all life, and created man perfectly in His own image, why is man now imperfect? Can you explain why and how the Great Spirit first found its lodgement in the firmament and why we humans could not?"

This is a question of the microcosm and macrocosm. Man possesses in latent form all aspects of perfection. But he has to achieve perfection, which is an infinite process. There is no difficulty here at all. Man is not created perfect in mind, spirit and body. But he is given the divine, perfect spark. It is for him to order his life so that the spark becomes a radiant flame.

The trouble with your world is that man creates God in his image. He thinks of the Great Spirit as not even a woman but a man. There are men who believe that being male is superior to being female. The Great Spirit created all humanity in its spiritual image. Life is spirit, and spirit is life. Because you are created in the divine image, you are forever linked with the Great Spirit, sharing the Great Spirit's divinity. As a corollary you are members of a vast spiritual family because all have the same essence of divinity within them. So it is a spiritual likeness, not a physical one.

The Great Spirit has been in charge of the universe for a very long time and knows exactly what is best. Do not worry. Do the best you can; that is all we ask of you.

You cannot change the world at once. Neither can you change people. You can change only yourselves. You are responsible for what you do and for nobody else. Help wherever you can. Serve wherever you can. Offer what you have received. If others will share it, rejoice. If not, let them go their way. Those you are to help will be brought to you.

The Great Spirit cannot be divorced from the world which divine love and intelligence created and exists only because the power of the spirit animates it.

The Great Spirit Must get very fed up with the people in it.

That is nothing new; it is very ancient history; but just as we try to teach tolerance so we have to practise it. If we did not love you we would not come back to a very dark world. It is only because we know we can help, when there are those ready to be helped. Alas, too often they have to experience the depths of spiritual despair before the soul can be touched and begin to be quickened into activity.

The light of the spirit will continue to illuminate wherever it can. In some lands it is only a flicker, but that light, because it is divine, can never be extinguished. There are natural laws which control and regulate not only your world, not only the universe, but the whole cosmos. The Great Spirit is competent enough to have made provision for all throughout the whole of the cosmos. Do not worry. It is a bad counsellor and never does anything to improve the situation.

Was Jesus a human who progressed through many incarnations? Did this begin man's acquisition of the etheric body? Or was he before the creation of earth?

All I can say is that the spirit power which expressed itself through the Nazarene is in essence exactly the same as the one expressing itself through everybody in your world today. There are differences of degree, of spiritual evolution, but there are no differences in the kind of spirit. All spirit is the same. It is possible for spirit to incarnate throughout the ages in many forms through many individuals.

Asked about prayer, the guide explained:

No prayer, no earnest, honest desire to strive towards greater efforts to extend the boundaries of knowledge, to heal more who are sick, and comfort more who mourn, to add a greater ray to your lighthouse that enables weary ones to find a path to you, all part of the task on which we are engaged, fails to get a response.

You are not alone. You are part of a vast army. Behind and beyond us there is a tremendous range of liberated beings of much higher development spiritually than you perhaps can appreciate. You and I, and others who work close to us, have access to this vast richness. The only limiting factor is our capacity to receive and to assimilate. As we unfold, so more of this divine beauty, radiance, grandeur, nobility and lustre can. be ours. This is the incentive for all of us to exhibit more and more of the innate divinity which is the heritage of birth in your world.

Hold your heads high. You can achieve far more than all the churches, synagogues, temples and chapels. You can exhibit the power of the spirit, which they cannot. They prefer the arid theology which has choked the spirit and prevented it from flowing into their midst.

A circle member asked, "Is it to the natural law that we should pray?"

No, you pray to the Great Spirit which is within and without. You strive through aspiration and attunement to establish closer unity with that power. Your prayer should always be a desire for more illumination, knowledge, wisdom and understanding. And that prayer will always be answered because the very fact of its petition is helping you to express the inner divinity.

The same questioner said: "Sometimes we know that other people in your world are helping in certain things. We do not pray to them. How do they become aware of our request?"

Sincere prayer finds its target. When you really pray, and I mean pray and not ask for something to be given to you, your prayer finds its target. If you were clairvoyant, you would see that round and about you there is always a host of beings because of a link that binds you, kinship and a mutual desire to serve in specified fields. When you pray you draw them closer to you.

The unfailing magnetic law of attraction works. You build with your prayer a bridge over which that answer can come. That is why I always say banish fear. Fear disturbs the physical and spiritual atmosphere round you and makes it difficult for help to come.

Do you wait until people have invoked God's help before trying to help them? Or do you simply leave them or help them irrespective of whether they have asked for help or not?

It is impossible because of the efficacy of natural law for anyone or any form of being to be forgotten in the divine scheme. The natural laws are so perfect that they embrace all. Nothing and nobody is outside them. You cannot be overlooked by the Great Spirit. Wherever you may be, you are still under the care and in the orbit of the natural law that encompasses each one of us.

Your needs are always known. If you pray, you will get the help that is available according to the mental and spiritual stage you have reached at that moment. What sometimes does help is to make your prayer audible rather than silent because in vocalising it you are helping to clarify what it is you are striving to achieve.

What about those who don't pray, and are in the depths of despair? Because they don't believe there is a God, is there no help for them?

It doesn't matter if you believe the Great Spirit has no existence. This will not trouble the Great Spirit. But would they get help? Here is someone incapable of prayer or believing, for various reasons, in God. Yet he is in terrible trouble and needing help. What happens to him?

The ability to receive help does not depend on a belief or disbelief in the Great Spirit. It depends on the stage of mental and spiritual evolution reached. This determines what you will receive because you are fitted to receive it. This is cause and effect, which is the natural law.

Is there a lot of truth in the Bible?

It is a mixture of divine truth and man's falsification.

When we talk of life after death to people who are religious, they often quote the Bible where it says we should not talk to the dead. What would be your answer?

It would be twofold. The Bible has been the subject of manipulation throughout the years. It consists of mistranslations, omissions and, as you know it, is only a copy of a copy of a copy. No one can produce the original manuscripts and say, "This is where it all began."

You cannot point to any statement in the Bible and say it is authoritative. There is no evidence that what is stated in the Bible has the imprimatur of divinity. There are many horrible things in the Bible, particularly in the Old Testament. There are accounts of deception, villainy, murder and violence that nobody can possibly regard as being a divine revelation.

According to the Old Testament, God, the Great Spirit, is responsible for behaving sometimes in a way no wicked tyrant would on earth. So because something is in the Bible it does not mean it is true. If it is true it has to be demonstrated beyond all shadow of doubt.

To these people of religion I would say: Let us accept that it is said you should not communicate with those who have died. Why, then, in the New Testament, does the Nazarene and three of his disciples have a seance on a mountain where there appeared to them Moses and Elias and communicate, although they had been dead for a long time. It is said that the injunction, "You shall not talk with the dead," came from Moses. Yet Moses was the one to return and talk. This must be a problem for the religionist.

"When my wife and I produce a child, what are we going to tell him on religious matters, especially when I am not completely convinced by the Christian faith and realise the truth in Spiritualism?" Silver Birch told the questioner:

This is not so difficult as it would seem. Your responsibility as a parent is to ensure that children should get the kind of tuition that will best help to nurture them, so that they unfold according to the true religion, rather than having to succumb to falsities which they accept at an early age when their mentality is plastic and exposed unthinkingly to what is said.

The result, as you know, is that what is accepted in very early childhood can become hardened and embedded in the subconscious mind so that it acts as a barrier and hindrance to the acceptance of truth at a later stage. One of the great problems we find when we try to give teaching to your world is the fact that individuals subconsciously resist because of the false teaching they received in childhood. They are indoctrinated and this takes a long time to be overcome.

What happens sometimes too is that there is a kind of

catharsis. The individual throws away everything, the good and the bad, in adult life, and indulges in a revolt against the whole of life. Your responsibility is to ensure, as far as you can, that no false teaching should be implanted into child minds.

Try to see that the children are taught the fundamentals of all known religions, what is common to them, to stress the golden thread through them all, so that in time they. will learn to disregard the incrustations of theology and seek the simple truths.

A person has been brought up in a certain religion. Should this be destroyed if he is not ready for a new interpretation?

This is difficult. Unfortunately children are what you call brainwashed. They have what are believed to be religious ideas-though they are not because they are theological. ones-implanted in their minds, which are plastic, when they are too young to question, and therefore are not resisted. And the plastic mind gradually becomes hardened in adult life. As time goes on they are not ideas that they hold, but ideas that hold them.

So this is difficult. What you must do is not attempt to destroy what is dear to others, but to offer alternatives in the way of knowledge. There are plenty of books to be read on the origins of religion. There are many alternatives to the religion of the Christian, the Jew, the Buddhist or the Muslim.

Your world is full of many religions, but there is only one God or Great Spirit. It must be obvious even to those, of lowly intelligence that the Great Spirit is neither a Christian nor a Jew-nor even a Spiritualist. The essence of being spiritual is to have compassion not only for humans but for animals. Without compassion, you lack spirituality.

One of the reasons why mediums and healers have to go through the mill is to learn compassion for others going through the mill. That is why the path of the instrument is always a hard and not an easy one.

And for administrators as well?

But it is worse for the instrument. So far as the administrators are concerned, when you are waging a war against materialism the privates have to be tried in the heat of the battle before they become generals. Be compassionate, not to destroy, but to point to other ways. It is not the hammer you should use on them, but any other tool that delicately suggests there are other ways.

If the soul is ready the attempt will be made. If the soul is not ready, unfortunately that individual is doomed to darkness on earth spiritually, mentally, and for a long time in our world as well.

Commenting on attempts to have unity in orthodox religions, Silver Birch said:

So they add chaos to confusion. But do they matter? They may think they are very important people, but where the gift and the light of the spirit cannot be expressed then their buildings are what the Nazarene called whited sepulchres. I do not think we need bother very much with those who cannot find common meeting ground because their rituals and doctrines divide them. The spirit unites always. It is man's outlook that divides. The spirit will work its unifying will whenever it is given a chance.

It is a matter of history that many years ago the power of the spirit operated to give birth to these religions which profess to follow in the same common stream, but they are tributaries that were diverted centuries ago. Let them go their way.

We will place our complete trust and reliance on the divine power that it will inspire people of good will to serve by utilising the gifts with which they are endowed, and by teaching mankind regeneration, individuals will save themselves and the world in which they live.

The power of the spirit does not flow through established churches. It flows through the multitudes of the children of the Great Spirit who are expressing the gifts which a supreme Creator, with divine wisdom, has implanted in them. It is the exercise of these gifts that will bring liberation and teach your world how to live.

Next came, "Would you define what you mean by religious tolerance?" This arose from a questioner who said: `I believe Silver Birch's teachings to be stamped with the same truth as is contained in other religions. But cannot his teachings be called dogmatic and intolerant, for example, that the universe is controlled by natural law, that this law is perfect and immutable?"

I have never made any claim to infallibility. I am a human being like you, expressing truths which should appeal to your reason. There is no implicit threat that if you reject them you will be subject to any punishment. All we say is this is truth as we have found it. We offer it to you for your examination; accept or reject as you will. We have no means of compelling you to accept what comes from our world.

If through any instrument you are told that which makes your reason revolt, then pay no heed to it. The Great Spirit has given you the gifts of reason and common sense to be utilised. The essence of dogma is to accept without reason. What we say is that you should test all spirit teaching by your intelligence. If it measures up to that strict examination accept it; if not reject it. How else shall we win, with offers of reward or punishment? No, we must win by love, by common sense and by finding that we can meet on common ground.

At another circle came the following:

Do not attempt to overlook the tremendous significance of

the work in which we are all engaged. We have to undo the centuries of superstition that have placed the minds of millions in thraldom and subjection.

This has made it almost impossible for them to understand simply the great truths which would free them, so that they could live, as they should, in an exhilaration of body, mind and spirit, and enjoy the richness that should be theirs once they understand who they are, what they are and where they are going. So you have difficulties, but they are good for you.

We have had to encounter vast difficulties to reach your world. We have overcome them in many places. Now the light of the spirit shines throughout your world. There is not even one country from which it is absent. It may be that those who are the instruments of the spirit have to work in secret and behind closed doors, but the work will go on because none can gainsay it.

So welcome your difficulties as a challenge to reveal the true mettle of the spirit, your divine armoury. You have potentially the greatest power in the world within you. There is no handicap, no obstacle, no difficulty so strong that you do not possess the inner power and can also call on a higher power to overcome them.

Theology was discussed by the guide who said it was unfortunate that there are millions of people-who are ignorant of spiritual reality.

They think the totality of life is that which can be cognised by physical means. As a result they believe life has no underlying or deep purpose. Unfortunately, too, people who should be. spiritual leaders in churches are just as ignorant as their congregations because they too are blind, deaf and dumb to spiritual reality. The power of the spirit does not operate in their churches because their religions are now theological doctrines which take priority as far as they are concerned.

Theology emanates from the mind of humans. The power of the spirit, because it emanates from the Great Spirit, is divine. Thus revelation always must take priority over theology.

In many lands education is compulsory. Children go to school to learn lessons in a curriculum designed for one specific purpose, so that they are educated to be ready for the life they have to live when they leave school. If they are wise, sensible children and learn their lessons, then when they are adults they can face with some understanding problems that are inevitable. If they have failed to learn their lessons they are not equipped for the life that faces them after school.

Your earthly life is a kindergarten of the spirit. Here you learn lessons to equip the spirit so that you come to our world prepared. As it is, we have far too many arriving here who are not ready and they have to be taught. It is much more difficult to teach them in our world as it is for you to teach adults who have not been to school.

When you know there is an after-life where you have to account for every action, it must or should change your outlook. It says in the Bible that the earth is the. Lord's and the fulness thereof. Once you have spiritual knowledge you can give it away, but you are not the poorer for doing it. If you have earthly riches and give them away, you are the poorer as a result. That is the difference.

But however much you accumulate earthly wealth you can never own it permanently. You can be only the custodians or trustees during your earthly lives. These riches can be lost; they can be stolen; they can sometimes diminish in value; they can tarnish; they can lose their beauty. Anyway you cannot have them forever. But spiritual richness once acquired can never be lost.

Because truth and faith are involved to some extent in religion, it is germane to include these comments:

Truth cannot be accepted until the soul is spiritually ready. This applies to all its aspects. Truth itself, being infinite, can never be acquired in its entirety except in eternity, which again is an infinite process. You cannot give truth to those who are not ready to receive it. There will always be confusion, arguments, debates and discussions, but this is to the good. Out of the welter will come truth to those who are ready. And the readiness is determined by their spiritual evolution, by the stage of their development. This each must accomplish for himself.

If I say to you it is a truth for some, and you answer, "I cannot believe it, I would not in any way be upset. J would love you just the same because I recognise that you are on earth to unfold, to use your reason, your common sense and to reject everything which does not make sense to you. If we cannot win you by reason, which we have enthroned as the final arbiter, then we will fail.

I seem to have come to that point in my life when I want to teach these things, but I find it difficult. When I speak in churches, or take people in groups, I realise this is the truth, the only way. Am I right in saying this is what I believe and leave it at that?

Yes, let them find their way.

So, if they reject it, it does not matter.

Truth will not be harmed because some reject it. They are not ready. You just wait and kindle the spark. That is all you can do. If they refuse to respond, you must be sorry for them.

Why is it that in spiritual organisations we have so many business and material things to consider and do? We choose business people to help us out of our problems. How are we going to get the spiritual teachers? We realise there is a spiritual famine.

Do you know your Bible? Let me quote some familiar

words to you. "Seek ye first the kingdom of God, and His righteousness, and all these things shall be added unto you." What do you think that means?

I would say you have to look for the spiritual side first. Perhaps we have been going the wrong way.

Spirit is king, matter is servant. Spirit comes before matter. When the spirit is right matter will be right. It is all a question of priorities. No worthwhile cause will suffer for want of money. But if the priority is to ensure the money is there first so that the spirit can function, it will not work that way.

We come back to you by manipulating matter. We.have to learn how to manipulate this inert, slow, sluggish force when our vibrations are quick and delicate. Some here in this circle will tell you that we can succeed in manipulating matter when it is necessary. May I mention another verse in your Bible? "The earth is the Lord's and the fulness thereof." Nothing material belongs to you. You cannot really own it. Even when you acquire it it does not belong to you. You are stewards during your earthly life. It belongs to the Great Spirit.

If the prime desire is to serve, what is needed will be forthcoming. There is none who serves the world of spirit who has not found that we render service for service. The natural law ensures that, and nobody is overlooked, nobody is forgotten. Trust the divine power and provide it with a channel to work its divine will.

You make it so simple.

It is simple. There are too many people in your world who are so clever at confusing the issues that their judgement becomes clouded. Then you require the simplicity of a child going straight to the heart of the problem. "Except ye become as little children." We have never failed those who serve. What is necessary will be forthcoming. We have been put to that test many times. We have access to the spiritual and material wealth that are necessary. You play your part; we will play ours.

I have had great help from you and your words of wisdom.

You are clairvoyant. I wish that your inner sight could be extended so that you could see some of the liberated beings who compose the hierarchy, the masters, those endowed with the task of ensuring that the divine plan fulfils itself. Then, never for a moment would you falter or allow any wavering fear to enter the threshold of your being. I have seen them. I know what has to be achieved.

I tell you with all the strength that I can command that all of you who strive to serve have access to the greatest power in the universe, one that is life itself. It is a responsibility. Use it diligently, wisely. Help all who come within your orbit. If there are some with whom you cannot share this knowledge, let them go their way. Continue with the task as you see it according to your light and conscience. Motive determines all matters. If the motive is right, no matter what happens you will emerge triumphant.

There are two important principles in life. One is knowledge, the other is faith. Faith without knowledge can be a. very weak and even broken reed, but knowledge with faith, that is an admirable combination. You have knowledge which has brought comprehension of life and its meaning.

You know it is only an infinitesimal part of knowledge that can be yours. Thus the element of faith must arise. But this is the faith founded on knowledge.. It is not the credulous faith, not the unreasoning faith, not the faith that insults intelligence, but the faith founded on knowledge, that because of knowledge it is right to have faith. That is important for you.

Others here have heard me say this before and they must be weary of the repetition, but it is still true. A platitude is still true even if it has been said many times. The repetition does not diminish from its truth. What I want to say is that you are finite beings living in a finite world. The amount of infinite knowledge you can receive is limited by the stage of development you have spiritually and mentally reached. What you have received you have tested and found is true. On that you must build and have faith on what is still to be revealed to you. This is not unreasoning faith, but founded on demonstrable fact.

It is one of the strange paradoxes that it takes a very long time for people in your world to wake up from their materialistic sleep. Yet when they do they are in a hurry. They want things to happen speedily. It cannot be done that way. Spiritual progress must be slow. It cannot be instantaneously done because there are no short cuts to it. Every step forward has to be consolidated before any advance can be made. Each successive step reveals another still to be trod.

Rest content on the foundation of what has been revealed to you. When questions arise, as they must, and when doubts come, as they do, and when difficulties raise their troublesome heads, be patient. Know that the power of the spirit is stronger than matter. There is no obstacle, difficulty or handicap that the power of the spirit cannot overcome if you provide the right conditions. Those armed with this knowledge can endure anything that the world offers, for it is powerless to harm one hair of their spiritual heads.

The churches owe their existence to the fact that the power of the spirit manifested in various ways. By its demonstration seeming miracles were performed. But they do not happen today. What is called the Holy Land is a spiritual desert, arid, with hardly one oasis to be found. Yet the laws of the Great Spirit have not changed. It was made holy as this ground is hallowed because the power of the spirit manifested there in sublime form. It is manifesting through you and bringing its tremendous beneficence.

I do not seek to condemn those who do their best in their religions, but they have nothing to offer a world in travail. Their creeds are barren; their dogmas are sterile; they are antiquated in their outlook, and the world is passing them by.

We are the heralds of the new world which must prevail so that there can be driven from your earth the greed, avarice and selfishness that form the malignant cancers in far too many places. We enthrone service as the greatest of all religions, mutual helpfulness, tolerance, compassion to all, human or animal, so that you can truly have, if you so desire, a kingdom of heaven on earth.

That is the task on which we are all engaged. When you get downcast, tired or depressed, because the woes of your world assail and enfold you, and you allow gloom to surround you, hold your heads high and remember that all of us are part of a great army of the spirit chosen to fight the greatest of all battles, waging war on the materialism that could destroy your world were it given full reign.

Do not allow despair to stay too long with you. We will not fail you. No cause for good will ever fail if we have the instruments through whom we can work. When it is necessary we will provide you with all the sustenance that .you require. Even in your inflationary days we will see that you will not suffer. It is a great work on which we are all engaged. We should know by now, as I have said many times, to serve is noble. Nobility comes through service.

The people of your world have to learn to save themselves through self-redemption. They have to learn it is only by applying the spiritual principles of co-operation and service that they will enjoy all the benefits which are essential in your world. And I do not mean only material benefits but mental and spiritual ones.

There has to be freedom of mind, body and spirit in your world. We are opposed to slavery whatever form it takes. Man must deliver himself from his own bondage. He must recognise that the spirit which animates him is the same one that gives life to every other being and creature in your world. The power of the spirit girdles them all, brings them all together and makes them one in the sight of the Great Spirit responsible for their being.

That is what is behind all the work we do, to bring awareness, spiritual awareness, of the realities of life. It will not be easily attained because these lessons are learned only through difficulty, crisis, sickness, bereavement and the afflictions – which make people despair, but are in reality the means by which they can find themselves.

So you have work to do, but plenty of time for it. . Behind us all is the power of the Great Spirit, the mightiest in the universe. You will have setbacks. The tide does not only flow, it also ebbs. But the power of the spirit will continue. It will never cease.

Where there is life there is spirit. Stagnation and inertia are our enemies because the power of the spirit cannot flow where they exist. You give us the channels and the power will flow through them. All we want is dedicated co-operators, not puppets to be manipulated, but willing demonstrators who will work with us as we will work with them.

Service is the coin of the spirit. Religion is service, or should be, otherwise it has no meaning.

A young visitor expressed her viewpoint in these words: "As you say we all derive from the one life force, which is God, surely if we take love and service as our aim, everything else falls into place? Do you think it is necessary for the average person to have all these deep philosophical teachings? If you get across to people this one fact and teach them to create their lives on God, to know more of the Great Spirit, a large number could understand this rather than appreciate Spiritualism or Christianity." Silver Birch told her:

What you say is very good in essence and nobody could disagree with it. But people are at differing stages of growth, unfoldment, development and evolution. What would be acceptable to one would be rejected by another. If they were at a uniform level then you could give them a uniform message.

To suggest to some that the Great Spirit is the epitome love and wisdom will be readily accepted. Others will dismiss it because they do not believe in the existence of God. So you must adapt your message to the individual according to the degree of his reception. To some the very simplicity of what you say would appeal; to others it would not do so. They would challenge you by pointing to the injustices of life, to the many contradictions, to the apparent suffering of the innocent, to the way in which the selfish seem to escape punishment. And then you get involved in laborious argument.

For that type of mind it is essential to have an incontrovertible demonstration of spiritual reality, such as the healing of one said to have been incurable. Then that person is compelled to recognise the existence of a non-material force which cannot be explained in ordinary terms, but gives evidence in itself of being directed by benevolence or love.

There is another important matter. Knowledge, wisdom and truth are infinite and so there is no limit to the amount that you can acquire. On the surface the theme of universal love may seem simple. Behind the surface it is very complex. It is only as more understanding comes that you are able to appreciate the need for the complexity.

The visitor commented: "In other words, it is necessary

to have all these various sects and religions throughout the world. Each gives something to people when they reach a certain standard. They perhaps find satisfaction in a religion that someone else would not." Silver Birch replied:

An infinite spirit must have an infinite number of manifestations. The whole of life is graduated. You are evolving all the time. The point at which you start is not the end. When you climb a rung you find there is another one above, or, if you like, you scale one peak and another comes into view. Humanity is composed of individuals at differing stages of growth. It is impossible to present them with one teaching that will appeal to all. You have to find what it is they are ready for.

To some it may be the philosophy you enunciate. Others might be able to combat it by presenting different arguments. These must have a demonstration to appeal to the senses, to be shown something which is supernormal, spiritual in its origin, but physical in its manifestation. But whatever gift is used, as long as growth begins it is all that matters.

Chapter Nine

YOUTH—"THE MORROW'S DIRECTORS"

"WHAT would you teach the teenage group we are going to lead at our church?" This question was put to Silver Birch by a young woman paying her first visit. She explained that though it was a Nonconformist church, she and her husband did not propose to give "set Christian Bible teaching." The guide replied:

I think the best approach is always to appeal to reason and logic because today's youth is in revolt. It feels the old have failed them by presenting a world of darkness. I would appeal to the reasonableness of the philosophy that is behind all that comes from our world. You need not use words like Spiritualism, occultism, the esoteric, or mystical. These are only labels.

Tell them about the difference between brain and mind, between matter and spirit, and show that already in their own make-up there is a superior, animating, directing principle at work which cannot be chemically analysed or dissected in any laboratory. All human beings are marvels of construction, with the most highly organised, intricate and complex machinery your world has ever known. Its many constituents work together in harmony to enable you, to live, move, and breathe. But in addition to the physical apparatus there is the inner, unseen, superior, thinking, controlling individuality.

Behind the surface there is the mind at work which can appraise, consider, weigh, reflect, analyse, judge and decide. This is not something physical. You express affection, friendship, love and sympathy. Intrinsically they are non-physical. You cannot measure love. You cannot weigh, see, taste, smell or hear it. Yet it is there, one of the greatest forces in your world which actuates people to deeds of heroism and self-sacrifice.

Ask your group members, who are unaware of the spiritual truths with which you are familiar, what is this mind? As it is obviously superior to the physical body, is there any reason to suppose that when the machinery ceases to function the controlling mind has also ceased to function? I think along those logical lines you could make a good start.

If you can interest any young people, seize the opportunity. Never mind the scoffing or ridicule. Among them there may be one or two where your words will fall on receptive soil. If this is not immediate, then in a little while the seeds you have dropped will begin to grow. And you will - have helped another soul . to find itself. We are always concerned, whenever we can, in bringing self-awareness and self-realisation to people so that they can begin to live aright. This is the whole purpose behind our mission. We have coming into our world far too many wrecks, ill equipped, unready for the life which they have to resume when they come here.

At another circle this question came, "How would you suggest we can get the young ones interested in spirit truths?" The guide advised:

I think the interest must be aroused not on the basis of trying to prove, they can achieve communication with people in our world because, generally speaking, youth has not endured the experiences, the soul-searching, heartbreaking experiences of physically losing ones they love. And so it is not with evidence for personal survival that you can attract the young.

I would say the appeal must be to reason and to intelligence, to offer them spiritual" truths which will appeal to their logical instincts, not to ask them to have faith, hope or belief, but to question everything we say on the ground of its being reasonable, satisfactory and showing that it has the hall-mark of truth.

I would tell them that they are part of a vast universal plan controlled by immutable natural laws. These ensure that all facets of being and activity of the phenomena of life, nature and human beings are controlled by these divine ordinances which have made provision for all that can possibly happen so that there is complete control by an overruling power.

I would say here are examples of law-governed occurrences. Here are cause and effect in operation showing that one follows the other in an unbreakable sequential order. There are no miracles, no need to abrogate natural laws because they work and are implicit in revealing that all is known beforehand.

Then I would say that, with the evidence others have received, all this demonstrates that while . they are on earth they are spirits with bodies, that matter is only a reflection of spirit which infuses life into the body. The body of itself has no dynamic, no vitality. All that enables it to move, to breathe, to act in any way is due to the energising spirit that makes it possible. That spirit is superior to matter; that spirit is king and matter is commoner; that spirit is master and matter is the serf; that spirit dominates, regulates, supervises and controls all.

Then I would add that an awareness of this vital fact has profound implications. These, when understood, must revolutionise all human thought and enable every individual to have the right perspective, the correct priorities,. and to ensure that as much attention is given to unfolding and developing the spiritual nature, which is permanent, as is devoted to maintaining the physical body which is only temporary. And I think intelligent youth would respond to that kind of approach.

A circle member asked this supplementary question, "Would you recommend they join a development circle?"

Not at first. I would recommend they join groups for meditation which would appeal to them more, so as to give the inner faculties a chance of expression.

Would not that rather make them join so-called mystics?

If they do then they will have taken the wrong turning. That is the choice their free will must make. You must allow them to unfold in their own way. When they are ready they will receive. When the pupil is ready the master comes.

Do you feel that present-day youth is being spoken to by the spirit world? Is this causing the impetuous spirit within the present generation to seek something, even if it does not know what it is?

Partly the troubles are due to the upheaval caused by the last war in your world. These upheavals make all thinking upside down. They lead to people changing their allegiance, turning their backs on the past and searching for ideas which they think are more in consonance with the circumstances that prevail.

Youth, by its very nature, must be demanding and impetuous. So, while turning its back on the conventional and orthodox, it seeks quicker means of achieving understanding of what is hidden by the veil of matter. The taking of drugs, attempts at speeded-up forms of meditation and even the violence, these are part of the breaking up of the old when youth seeks the new.

The young must not be encouraged, of course, to believe that there are any hasty methods of achieving spiritual development. This is not possible. The prizes of the spirit cannot be earned in a flash. They have to be laboured for. Spiritual mastery involves a great discipleship. The student must realise that to attain the highest means a long dedication.

Youth should be encouraged to seek what lies beyond matter. Once youth appreciates that the veil, the material world, is the shell, and that the reality is behind and above the shell, then this will give a new impetus to life. The young can then make their contribution to the world in which they live.

Might I ask you about this rebellion of the young against organised society? Do you agree that possibly they are much more attuned to the other world and are responding to guidance from it without knowing it?

I don't mind the revolt. It is the violence to which I object.

The young are seeking a God based on love. Their ideas are based on love. They are not church-conscious but Godconscious. Is that right?

It is youth's function to revolt. If youth accedes it would cease to be youth. Youth must quest, search, rebel. You have had cataclysmic upheavals in your world which have changed convention and caused the loss of respect for established teaching.

Do not blame the young because they seek to find what they think are better ways of governing the world in which they live. But what is essential is an understanding that the whole of life is based upon spiritual and not material realities. Matter has no existence of itself. Matter derives its existence from spirit. Matter is the shell, the husk, spirit is the kernel.

Your bodies die because they are material and spirit has withdrawn. The great lesson for all in your world, young and old, is the realisation that spirit is the foundation of all life. It is only in the application of spiritual principles, in the expression of divine qualities, compassion, mercy, co-operation, tolerance, service, that you will achieve a greater measure of peace and fulfilment in your world.

It is the materialistic gospel, the enthronement of greed and selfishness that is responsible for the disasters that befall you. You have to replace greed with altruism. You have to replace selfishness with sacrifice. You have to ensure that those who are gifted should help the ones who are not gifted. This is the way in which ultimately there will come' into your world a greater measure of peace, harmony and compassion. than exists at present.

No, I am not pessimistic. I am optimistic. To use one of your sayings, the ball is at your feet.

You seem to be criticising what the young make of the society they are in, that they are interested only in the material, in more money and more status.

I am not blaming the young; . they have inherited the world. They are not responsible for its present condition. But they have also inherited much for which they have so far contributed nothing: In clays gone by pioneers and reformers of many kinds laboured to serve their fellows and left a rich legacy behind them.

The picture is not one of unrelieved gloom. Of course, man is spoiling much of the world in which he lives, but that is only part of the story, There are others, many others, who are striving to make their contribution, to bring enlightenment and wisdom and ensure that future generations will enjoy more of the richness of being because of the work that they do.

When I see my children, especially those growing up, needing guidance which they won't necessarily accept from me, it would be a comfort to know I could do something to expedite this.

It is very difficult. There are no short cuts in these matters. You can withdraw, meditate, become more receptive, which helps to ensure a closer contact with all those from our world who are round and about your family circle.

Is it really a question of creating the environment?

They will not listen to you easily because, being young, they think they know better. This is part of the normal process of your earthly' world. When you were young you thought you knew better than your parents. You must accept the fact that it is part of the natural growth of children to question authority. You must set them the example and give the reason for it. This is the only way. They have to accept that certain paths should be followed because it is in their spiritual interests to do so. But this is not easy for them.

It is difficult to make people believe in the things we know to be true. Could not the spirit world somehow make a concerted effort at this time, when it is needed so badly, to prove to people who won't accept these truths? Or is it not the right time?

No, it is not the right way. We are not interested in any attempts at mass-conversion, usually conducted in an emotional atmosphere which evaporates the next morning. Our purpose is different. We want people, one by one, to become convinced through their own inquiry and to be satisfied that all we present neither makes their reason revolt nor insults their intelligence.

We have to win them by demonstration and by logic. This we cannot do until they are spiritually ready. They cannot be spiritually ready until their soul has been touched by some crisis, tragedy or illness, which makes them realise that nowhere in the world of matter can they find answers to their questions. There is a saying in your world to the effect that man's extremity is God's opportunity.

This is the only way we can work. We believe that the individual, who is convinced beyond any shadow of doubt of the truth of spiritual realities, becomes aware of himself and his divine potential. He knows that life is continuous in an unbroken sequence after death. This soul who is aware will then begin to fulfil himself. He will order, or should do, his life in the light of the knowledge, so that he expresses more and more of the divinity within and grows in spiritual and mental stature and grace.

It is your duty, having knowledge of these matters, to offer it to those who come your way. But it is no use banging your head against stone walls by trying to convert the unreceptive. You should always be available to help those who come to you. If you help them, express gratitude for being able to do so. If you cannot help them, shed a tear, for they have had their chance and they failed to take it.

There is no other way because that. which is easily gained will be just as easilyy lost. The path to spiritual attainment is long, slow and difficult. The prizes of the spirit can be earned only by arduous labour and sacrifice.

There is no short cut, no instant method of gaining spiritual superiority. The soul has to earn it by a life of exertion. Otherwise the law would be cheated if the selfish man could attain overnight all the qualities that have taken long years for the saint to achieve. This indeed would be a mockery of divine justice. Each soul must accomplish its own growth, development and evolution. This ensures that once conviction comes, the soul can no longer be unaware of the truths of the spirit.

There is no need to be downhearted. We are making progress, we are winning, not losing. It is the forces of confusion that are in disarray. The truths of the spirit march forward all the time. It was sorrow which brought you this knowledge. You were receptive because you had almost reached the very depths of despair. But you would not turn back now.

And that is how it will be for others. We rejoice at the gradual but inevitable spread of these great truths as more and more become receptive, awaken from their long slumber and begin to live as the Great Spirit intended they should.

What you consider important are sometimes regarded by us as trivial. And what you regard as trivial to us can be important. It depends on where the standpoint happens to be. In terms of fractions, 70 over infinity is not very large.

Just as it was a blinding light on the road to Damascus that changed Saul, so it can be that one incident is the catalyst for providing the soul with the means to begin to come into its own. It depends on the factor. I cannot lay down any hard and fast rules. The primary purpose of all earthly incarnation is for the soul to come into its own. If the soul is not touched, then earthly existence is a waste of time. The soul has not had the opportunities for the education which earthly life provides.

What happens to the souls who are not touched here on earth?

This is very difficult. It is akin to what happens to adults who face life without having had any education of any kind. They start with complete unawareness. They are the misfits in your world and in ours. It means they have not learned the lessons that should equip them for our life. They are unready, unprepared.

How can you help them?

Some of them have to incarnate again into your world because we cannot do very much for a soul who has no awareness. It can take hundreds of years as you measure time to bring that awareness to them.

Are they helped by their spirit friends?

As much as they can be helped. But until awareness comes there is darkness. Without awareness light cannot penetrate. This is a primary problem that confronts us.

Is it their fault?

This is not a good word. Let me answer it in my way. To every individual in your world there comes an opportunity to attain self-realisation. The Great Spirit is perfect. Nothing is forgotten, neglected, overlooked and nobody can be outside the orbit of the natural laws. These make provision for every soul to have the chance of self-awareness.

When you call it "fault," I have to say the chance has not been taken. You have heard me say many times that when people come to you and you cannot heal them or help them, feel sorry for them. It is a chance they have lost. It is not your fault. You can only do the best for them. If they cannot accept it, say a silent prayer for them.

If you try to help them and they do not respond, you must let them go. They must not be chains around your neck. Every soul during its earthly incarnation gets the opportunity of learning truth and finding itself. If it rejects it, do not blame yourself. Your responsibility is to discharge your duty to the best of your ability. When you have done that, forget it and try to help the next one who comes. This is not being ruthless. The power of the spirit must not be frittered away for those who cannot measure up to it.

When Silver Birch greeted a young girl from New Zealand whose parents work for Spiritualism, he said:

I always tell newcomers that I have to try to live up to the picture painted of me because I am not all-wise as might be inferred from the way in which my teachings are presented to your world. I have been able to learn something about eternal truths and am willing to share my knowledge with those ready to receive them.

This is what matters, they must be ready to receive. Truth cannot enter closed minds. Truth can find a lodgement only when there is an ability to receive it. Truth, like the Great Spirit, is infinite. The amount you can receive depends on your capacity. If you increase your capacity you can receive more truth. You can never reach the stage that you know everything about the universe in which you dwell.

That is a long preamble. But I always tell young people like yourself how fortunate you are to be the recipient of this knowledge at an early age because it can be so helpful in your unfolding life. How sad it is to see so many youth still being taught falsehood, so that their minds are cluttered up with ridiculous notions in the name of religion. They are of no value to them and furthermore act as a hindrance rather than a help to their evolution.

Doctrines made by man, and not the Great Spirit, are implanted in tender minds which cannot resist them. In too many cases in adult life they repeat in parrot fashion these teachings which become part of the subconscious fabric of their being. That makes it all the more difficult for them to receive the truths of the spirit which would be of inestimable benefit to them.

I think it is fair to say that one of the great curses in your world has been the constant dissemination of theological, meaningless doctrine which has caused division instead of unity, which leads to bloodshed, violence, conflict, wars and separation, instead of being the foundation on which all can unite in recognition of their common spiritual nature.

So I say how fortunate you are to be aware of these spiritual truths. You can face the great adventure of life knowing its purpose and realising that you are part of a tremendous plan conceived by infinite love and wisdom. This is your most priceless possession. This is the spiritual armoury with which you are equipped.

You can face the battles of earthly life and know that whatever experiences befall you, you are in possession of a power to enable you to conquer difficulty, to override obstacles and grow in spiritual grace and beauty and strength. Then you can make your contribution.

The Great Spirit is unity in diversity. Every human being is different, yet fundamentally they are the same because the same spirit animates them. But they are diverse and no two are completely alike. Each is endowed with a gift which, when developed, can enable its owner to help some people less fortunate.

You have gifts, as everyone has, which it is your responsibility to develop. I am not necessarily referring to gifts of the spirit. I am referring to other talents that all human beings possess and which give them the means of enriching the world. How radiant it would be if all its occupants were able to exercise the gifts and talents with which they have been endowed.

This is the great promise that the morrow holds for all of you as you help to dissipate the gloom, fog and darkness, the superstition and error, the ignorance and falsity which lie like a cloud of miasma all over the earth. But here and there are the little lighthouses of the spirit "reflecting beams of truth, showing the way so that some pilgrims can emerge out of the darkness and learn to find themselves and become aware of who and what they truly are. You can go forward fearlessly. With this knowledge as your base you can look forward to an exhilarating earthly life.

A different aspect of youth and its problems came at another session:

These young people are not easy. If I may say so, when you were young, none of you was easy either. But as you get older you tend to forget your youthful rebelliousness. You were quite sure that all the older ones had made a mess of the physical world. It was now the duty of youth to put it straight.

As they get older and understanding comes, they realise there is much for which they should be grateful because of what was done for them without any effort on their part. All this is part of the polarity and balance of life in which youth and age play their respective parts because they are complementary to one another just as men and women are.

The whole scheme of life is perfectly balanced, so that when all works in proper concord a true harmony is achieved. So it becomes appropriate that those who are older in physical years should exercise a good humour, a toleration for the young who have still to learn many lessons that the older ones have already assimilated.

Discussing the young with a visiting healer Silver Birch said:

The leaven is at work; it is fermenting and they do not know where to turn. They are searching, questing, seeking, dissatisfied with the sterility of conventional teaching. They are drawn, sometimes unconsciously, to the spiritual, mystical, the unseen and intangible. Their souls cry out for the satisfaction that only the things of the spirit can give. But they are confused, they are in a hurry because they are young, and they want instant development, instant satisfaction.

"Thus heroin and LSD," said the guest.

One must be tolerant. One must understand and try to help them. If you can effect a lodgement of spirit power within them to ignite that spark, then you have performed a tremendous task. It can make the greatest difference to the whole of their earthly lives.

The healer said he had found that many young people on LSD were becoming possessed by harmful entities.

Unfortunately some of these drugs open a psychic centre that can reach out no higher than the lowest astral field surrounding your earth. The beings who can invade them are like themselves, often drug addicts, or alcoholics seeking satisfaction because their unevolved state chains them. They are not free. The healing power is the catalyst. This can help to clarify the whole complex situation created by physical, spiritual and astral conditions getting mixed up. Once you get harmony between spirit, mind, and body then health begins to be achieved.

Another time came the vital comments:

The young are the ones who will be the directors of the morrow. If their thinking can be guided aright, so that they get the true perspective on their lives, then they can play their important part in helping peace to be more firmly established.

Chapter Ten

ANIMALS—OUR FELLOW BRETHREN

YEARLY millions of animals throughout the world undergo horrific experimentation by their "civilised" caretakers-man. If there is a worse spiritual crime than inflicting deliberate harm on a fellow man or woman, it is cold bloodedly abusing humanity's fellow creatures of the animal kingdom. Does it ever occur to the hordes of white-coated, blood-stained experimenters, scientists and researchers that man also is simply an animal? Because of the wider vision and responsibility that Spiritualism bring, many Spiritualists are prominent animal welfare crusaders.

If, as you say, the law is perfect, why is it that a large proportion of the animal world, fulfilling natural law, can survive only by causing appalling suffering to other living creatures?

Yes, the law is perfect, even when you fail to understand its manifestations. A long experience has shown me that there are no imperfections in natural law. It is conceived by infinite wisdom and sustained by infinite love. As you have heard me say many times, it has made provision for every facet of creation and ensures that nothing or nobody is ever forgotten, uncared for or overlooked.

Evolution, part of this law, is a constant progress from lower to higher forms of being and activity. In its lower animal forms it outworks itself by what is seemingly cruel as these animals prey on one another. Through evolution these predatory instincts gradually vanish. If you look at prehistoric times the greatest of all predators have disappeared from the physical scene, while those animals not involved in preying on one another have survived.

There is another aspect to be considered. In some respects the animal creation reflects its human counterpart. As man evolves and manifests less cruelty to his fellows, so this will be reflected in the animal kingdom.

A circle member commented, "I have noticed there are animals who are ahead of their own natural species and exhibit more human qualities."

This must be true because in all the outworking of evolution there are those who are the pioneers showing what will be achieved in the future, just as there are the laggards who have not even caught up with what should be the normal expression of evolution for their species.

In human activity you get the genius, the reformer and the saint who exhibits qualities of his spiritual nature and by his gifts he can show what your world of tomorrow could be like. Similarly there are animals who have gone some stages ahead of the others and exhibit qualities that can often compare with the finest examples of heroism and service that humans can offer.

If the reason for life is to learn love and compassion, why does nature set such a bad example by allowing predators?

Nature does not set anyone a bad example. Nature is an expression of the Great Spirit. The Great Spirit is perfect. The laws of the Great Spirit are perfect. Nature left to its own devices will always achieve the right balance and harmony. If man lived in harmony with nature then your world would be a paradise, a kingdom of heaven.

There are predators, but that is part of the way nature ensures the survival of the fittest. Yet that is only one aspect of.natural law at work. The essence of nature is co-operation.

Nature is symbiotic. You, for example, are a gardener. If you prepare your garden and co-operate with nature, the results are beautiful. Man is the predator in your world, the greatest destructive creature that has been known for many millions of years.

Another question came from a woman who, saying she had a great respect for all life, asked, "Is it wrong to spray with insecticides to try to prevent malaria, sleeping sickness, etc?"

Of course you must have respect for all life, but this is a question of motive and of degree. If you have conditions where, due to certain circumstances, there are. the kind of insects that cause disease, then your motive in using sprays is a good one. Respect for life must be tempered with the necessity of ensuring there are conditions in which it can flourish. Similarly if you have houses infested with bugs, it is easier to spray and get rid of them if your motive is to improve the health of those who dwell there.

If an animal on earth develops human qualities, such as noble sentiments and intelligence, will it remain an animal without any chance of further evolution, or may it in time step into the human realm?

Evolution is part of a natural law. It has a mainstream and many tributaries, but all are part of the same law. The spirit within you is in essence the same spirit within the animal. There is no difference in essence but only in degree. Potentially, being infinite, the spirit can achieve the tremendous expression latent in man or animal, but . spiritually it is all part of one path. Who is to determine where spirit has branched off to be expressed through an animal, as distinct from branching off to be expressed through man? I do not see the problem there at all.

Does an animal evolve in a similar way to man?

It follows its own path of evolution. It is part of the same pattern which is behind all evolution; it is a development. If I say to you, "Do all children evolve in the same way as their parents?" the answer is "Yes" and "No." They have a predestined pattern which they must follow, but within that there is a certain amount of free will regulated by the awareness reached at stages of unfoldment. Everything which has spirit is capable of infinite development.

After listening to comments made by circle members the guide said:

Animals follow their line of evolution according to the part they play in the whole process. The law of cause and effect is immutable. Whatever is must be the result of what was. The animal is an essential part of the evolutionary plan, just like the tree, the ocean and everything in nature.

The link is the unifying spirit. All life is one. You have a relationship not only with animals but with all wherever there is life. They will follow their preordained paths. The extent to which they develop is governed by that part of the law which applies to them, as it applies to a flower, a tree, a bird, to the beasts of the field or to a human being.

Can an animal therefore break its own law?

Only in.a sense that you contravene a law, but it will operate just the same. You can transgress, but you cannot break the law in the sense of preventing effect from following cause. You can only kick over the traces.

Could an animal ever do anything for which it can be blamed spiritually?

Yes, if it transgressed the operation of natural law. There are rogue animals just as there are rogue human beings.

Would the individual animal know it had broken the law?

I do not know. I am not an animal. You must have the good and the bad. No animal, no human, nothing is perfect in your world.

If a human is bad he has a conscience. If an animal is a rogue animal there are reasons.

It is still subject to the law of cause and effect. I cannot alter the law.

It has been said by many guides that when an animal dies it returns to a group soul. However there is considerable evidence for animal survival. Could you enlighten us on this apparent paradox?

There is individual survival for domestic animals that have had association with humans. Thus they have been helped to achieve an individual evolution that is not possible with animals who are still in a group soul, or soul group, even on earth.

It is part of the wonderful relationship that can exist between humans and animals, each helping the other to develop spiritually. You help the animal that comes into your surroundings to achieve a consciousness that is more personal and individual than it otherwise would have been. It is that which survives death. But where there is not this more evolved "human" expression it joins the soul group or group soul.

This led again to a circle member's comment: "I feel that as humans develop under present circumstances and know more and more about animal life, this too will help the animals. This is so because we have proved that kindness affects animals. If you are kind to a wild baby animal it has demonstrated in many cases that it grows to have human characteristics."

"This is because all life is one," said another member. Silver Birch replied:

These are all branches of the evolutionary tree. These are all developments of the evolutionary pathway. In all such matters kindness produces kindness, compassion produces compassion, love produces love and hate produces hate. So you must follow the highest ideals. In doing so you are helping one another in your evolution, the animal and the human, because all life is one life. There are physical divisions, but spiritually all are one.

A third member asked, "Would an animal reincarnate?"

No, though there is a theory about the transmigration of souls.

When the animal is no longer in contact with the person who is the cause of its progress, does it then slowly begin to return to the group soul, or alternatively is it in a kind of. limbo?

All the animals associated with you will be there to greet you when you come here. They will stay with you as long as it is necessary to do so, because you have helped them to gain an individuality that cannot be dissolved and this will be perpetuated. It is the individuality that persists.

Is it the intention that all such animals shall gain this individuality in association with human beings, that all animals shall have consciousness in their own right?

Yes, as man radiates love in his thinking and his actions towards all the animals, then in return they will radiate love and, as it says in your Bible, about the wolf and the lamb, man will lie down with them at the same time.

In order to sustain life, man has no alternative but to take plant life, filch fowls' eggs and cows' milk or, more savagely, slaughter animals. How can such imperative, robber sustenance be reconciled with an all-beneficent Creator without offence to that reason which you, often enough, have bidden us not to disregard?

Don't blame the Creator because you kill animals. The choice is yours. You do not have to kill them,, but in any case the answer is very simple. Your evolution will decide for you what you should do in all these matters. If you have any doubts your conscience will give its added answer.

You are responsible for what you do, and all your actions

will affect your spiritual nature. An added factor is your motive. If your motive is clearly good and you have to kill, then that obviously produces an ameliorative result in your development.

You cannot cheat the spiritual laws because they are based on cause and effect, reaping and sowing. Everything you do, think and say has an automatic, inflexible result; no cheating is possible. If you do wrong consciously then you are responsible for it. Your shoulders must bear the burden that results.

If you do good because you desire to do so, not for vanity's sake, because the motive then is poor, but because your soul desires to serve, then by the very fact of that happening you must be spiritually better for it. This is the law that will always operate.

I have always said that it is preferable not to be involved in consuming food that bears the mark of Cain upon it. Killing is wrong, though sometimes motive must of necessity be taken into account.

Those who desire spiritual mastery must be prepared to pay the price and live in harmony with the natural laws of the universe. These are spiritual in origin. The aspects of the spirit are always the same, love, compassion, tolerance, sympathy, co-operation. If you follow these principles you will find you are being led to eat aright, to drink aright, to live aright. But yours is the responsibility for, deciding because the Great Spirit has endowed you with the gift of free will.

Perhaps you would like to say something about the latest problems in what they call animal farms. Antibiotics and other drugs given to animals are finding their way back into the people that eat their flesh.

It is part of nature's eternal cycle that if you inflict suffering on others you must pay the price for it. You cannot be cruel to others and escape the result of your cruelty. If, because of greed, and for no other reason, you imprison the animals and deprive them of their natural rights, then you are creating a vicious circle. The law of cause and effect operates with the result that you must suffer. Only through compassion, love, mercy, kindliness and co-operation do you achieve the best that the whole of nature has to offer, whether it be animal, vegetable, flower, bird or human.

Are we on the verge of discovering that we cannot help people through what we call vivisection? When that is understood, will that mean a great advance in our moral and spiritual life?

I would say that you can help people through vivisection, but it is not right to do so because it is contrary to everything spiritual to inflict cruelty and suffering on creatures who have done nothing to deserve it.

Man is responsible for what he does. His motive may be good in many cases and that will affect his spiritual, development. That is how the law works. But it is not part of the divine plan that the children of the Great Spirit should become healthy through exploitation and cruelty to the animals in your world. This is so obvious that it requires no emphasis so far as I can see.

This is where the doctors have taken the wrong path. They justify themselves by saying that man is more important than the animal. Therefore he has a right to improve his health and well-being by experimenting on these creatures. But that is wrong.

The law is co-operation. Responsibility should engender mercy and compassion. You cannot exploit others without your suffering as a consequence. Exploitation is harmful to the exploiter. Cruelty is bad for the one who performs the cruelty. When you manifest love you are the better for it. When you manifest hatred you are the worse for it. This is how the natural law works.

It is right to strive to lessen the cruelty inflicted on animals, to show there is a better way, a way of mercy, that by teaching people how to order their lives aright, to live in harmony with the natural law, they will become well, healthy and radiant.

What is wrong spiritually can never be condoned. But in an imperfect world there will always be abuses and excesses. You must fight to promote the welfare of all who should dwell together in amity, peace, concord and love. For love is the fulfilling of the law. You cannot have love if you wreak cruelty on others.

The Nazarene laid it down that the greatest expression of love was to direct it towards your enemies. This is not easy. It is easy to love those for whom you feel affection, sympathy and kinship. But if you can love those who possibly may often be your enemies, then this is the highest manifestation of the divine. It always must be that the things that are worth while are the most difficult to do.

If it was easy to attain spiritual advancement, it would not be worth the having.

Probably a small advance is to wish our enemies well, which is as. ar as most of us can go.

Yes, but it must always be our task to direct you to express love, compassion and tolerance. These are the qualities of the spirit. As they manifest your world becomes better. So, you must go on doing the best you can. If you help one person, or one creature, it is worth while.

You have said that f the spirit is right then the material things will naturally follow and be right. How does that apply to animals in this world who are being born to be tortured, slaughtered and misused generally by man? Surely their spirit is right.

No, that is not in the same category as the human spirit because man is given the responsibility of making the right choice; that is his free will. Man has the power of helping or hindering the evolutionary plan. Thus he has free will to decide, within limits, how he treats those who share the planet with him. Your World is full of many abuses. Not the least among them is the needless cruelty to animals and their exploitation. But it cannot be otherwise if man is to progress. Were he deprived of his free will he would not have the chance to evolve his individuality and develop. So this is the crux of the whole matter.

It is so difficult for us to understand how this is allowed to happen.

If you use the words "allowed to happen" it means you would rather humanity was robbed of its free will. I repeat that if humans are deprived of their free will they cease to be anything but puppets and are unable to unfold the divinity within them. Their spiritual natures will not evolve and the whole purpose of earthly life will be missed. You are put on earth because life is the nursery, the school, the training ground for the spirit. The spirit can evolve only when it is exercised by meeting challenges and overcoming them.

A circle member joined the discussion by saying: "It does seem unfair to our mortal, human minds that because mankind is learning and sometimes making bad mistakes, the corollary must be the ones that pay are defenceless animals. It seems there is something amiss where man does the wrong things and the animals pay."

How else would you have it?

"One would think that if a man did something wrong, then retribution would be on his head rather than on an animal."
Silver Birch answered:

There is the law of compensation and retribution. You are affected spiritually and automatically by whatever good or wrong you do. None escapes the law of cause and effect. Compensation and retribution are intrinsically parts of the natural law. There is compensation for those animals on whom cruelty is wreaked, just as there is compensation for those who suffer from the despotic acts of humans in your world for which they are not responsible.

Another circle member said, "I do not think man will ever be other than cruel to animals."

No, that is not necessarily so.. There will be a gradual awareness of man's responsibility to other forms of creation. I do not say there will come a time when overnight cruelty will finish. You are evolving in an evolving world. There will be heights and depths, rises and falls, because evolution is spiral in its effect. But the overall picture is a gradual shift towards progress, otherwise there would be no evolution. You must recognise that the plan is devised, by infinite wisdom and love, so that provision has been made for everything and everybody.

Yet another circle member joined in: ` I was going to say it is our fault that animals are being treated cruelly. Gradually human beings are learning they must not eat them." To this a visitor added: "I wish it were evident to man when he acted cruelly. He seems to get away with it." The guide countered:

Nobody gets away with it, to use your parlance. The law will always fulfil itself. If you cannot see the results in your world, I assure you they obtain in ours. You cannot in any way alter the law of cause and effect. This law is immutable, inevitable, mathematical in its operation. Effect must follow cause.

Nobody gets away with it. If people could, then the Great Spirit would cease to be the perfect justice that the Great Spirit is. There is another aspect which I always stress. It is that unfortunately you can only have the shortterm, not the long-term, view. You see only what happens in your world, but the results are outworked in ours.

"We are impatient," said the visitor.

That we know. Do the best you can to awaken responsibility in others. Help to bring nearer that time when the wolf shall lie down with the lamb. Evolution must fulfil itself.

"If we as humans were able to live more the natural, divine way of life, thousands of animals would not be subjected to experimentation," said another guest.

That is true. We must persist in our efforts to spread enlightenment and truth wherever we can. Every time we break down a barrier we must rejoice. The power of the spirit works by evolution, not by revolution. The people of your world must pay the price for divorcing themselves from nature and all its great powers which are locked within its recesses.

Man is a spiritual being with spiritual attributes, spiritual potential, spiritual capabilities. Man. has the power so to order his life that he is able to help others, particularly the animals, to evolve as well as himself The plan must fulfil itself. Man can hinder and delay, but he cannot prevent it from coming into operation.

Animals are said to be our "lesser brethren." Is it true that they are less developed than humans and have not yet reached our stage of evolution? I am thinking for example, of the selfless devotion and patience of dogs. Surely we could learn from them. Are they on a different path from ours?

No, evolution embraces all life. There is only one law of evolution for all facets of life. Words are always difficult. When you use the phrase, "the lesser brethren," it is suggested animals have not achieved the stage of awareness that humans have. And it implies this must be so because they are not endowed, as humans are, with all the mechanism for reason, understanding, judgement and for decisionmaking and to a large extent they are controlled more by instinct. So it is suggested they can be considered lesser from one point of view. But that is not the ultimate test.

Of course there is much to learn from animals. They express qualities of fidelity, devotion, helpfulness, sacrifice and dedication which are excellent examples for humans to copy. But, then too, humans are also capable of expressing these qualities, and even to a greater degree, because their consciousness has evolved to a higher state, not a higher spiritual state, but a higher one than animals.

A circle member said, "Many people now dislike the word 'lesser' and say 'younger'."

I think that is a much better description.

"We have so many wonderful stories of animals doing far better things than humans," the same member said.

"And some animals are psychic, added another.

That is part of the law of compensation which always operates. When there is a deficiency of one faculty there is a compensating faculty. Thus the blind man gets an increasing sensitiveness that ordinary people do not possess.

A lot of people ask if cats who live in homes are aware of spirit entities when human beings are not.

Of course they are. This is due to the fact that your civilisation, as it is sometimes mistakenly called, has compelled people to live further away from nature than they should. They are divorced from all the power and strength that nature brings. Thus their psychic faculties have become more inhibited than races who lived and still live closer to nature and all its tremendous resources.

Domestic animals, generally speaking, have not had the "benefits" of your civilisation. Their natural psychic faculties are functioning more than the humans who are allegedly called their masters. And they have a natural awareness of people from our world that unfortunately most human beings do not possess.

Animal welfare was also mentioned when the guide spoke to a bereaved husband whose wife had laboured in this field:

Your wife says she is pleased with you because you have continued the task which was the whole of her earthly life and in which you shared, playing your part in helping to end needless, foolish and wicked cruelty to animals. These are blots, foul stains on what is called civilisation. Those of you who are aware of the oneness of all life must never weary in the struggle to ensure that animals regarded as lesser beings should have the fulness which is their right.

Continue your challenge to oppression, cruelty, torture and needless shedding of blood. Help to play your part in this worthwhile struggle in which ultimately good will overcome man's folly.

For too long, this man commented, it was unfortunate that those who practised cruelty seemed to be on the winning side.

Good will triumph over evil, just as light will triumph over darkness. The power of darkness cannot triumph over light, neither can the power of evil triumph over good. Never lose heart. You have at your side many whose earthly lives were devoted to these causes and who continue to co-operate to ensure that freedom should come to all who dwell in your world.

The plan is there. You have the great privilege of helping to share in it so that it can be fulfilled, as ultimately it will be. Man can thwart, man can delay, man can hinder, but man cannot overrule the plan of the Great Spirit.

Silver Birch was told, "What I cannot understand is the lack of unity in people who are supposed to be fighting these cruelties while those on the Other Side present a solid front."

Unity is very difficult to achieve. Unfortunately in your world personalities often take priority over principles. People engaged in good causes tend, as time goes on, to forget them and to think of self. This is a human problem. It exists largely through the lack of spiritual understanding.

They are dedicated to the causes they serve only if they can be achieved their way, they say. In their vanity they believe that theirs is not only the right way but the best and the only one. This. is one of the problems that causes dismay to those in our world who spent their earthly lives in championing these same causes.

What you have to do-it is not easy-is to get these people to understand they must try to forget their personality clashes, concentrate on the fundamental principles on which they should be engaged and work selflessly for those causes to which they were attracted first. It is not only true in the sphere of service in which you are engaged. It is true in other spheres.

Is it not true that in the movement called Spiritualism you have the same problem of people refusing to submerge personalities and there are clashes due to vanity? I say to you that no effort for good is ever wasted. Gradually these fights will be won because the power that is behind you is such that it cannot be halted. However great the opposition it will be forced to retreat.

Reform is not only inspired from our world, it has the blessing and co-operation of enlightened beings who bring great power to bear. You must always be urged to continue to fight for the things that matter. Never become weary in well doing. This is important. Keep a stout heart. There is plenty you can do. You are acquitting yourself well. When things are most difficult the way will be shown.

I cannot recall any difficulty that has come to any of you which has been insurmountable. Sometimes you have to wait until the 59th minute for help to come to you, but it comes.

The most beautiful rose is surrounded by thorns. Beauty emerges out of seeming dirt. There is a pattern, a polarity, a diversity, a corollary always to be observed in the working of natural law. Depth and height, sunshine and storm, ignorance and knowledge, war and peace, love and hate, error and truth, weakness and strength, each has its part to play.

Evolution cannot work in any other way. In your weakness you will find strength. In your darkness you will find light. In difficulty you will find help. It is platitudinous but still true to say that the darkest hour always precedes the dawn. This is part of the paradox of all being. This is how evolution is able to achieve its immutable purpose.

With this knowledge there should never be any need for sorrow, for thinking the powers-that-be do not know what they are doing. There are factors of which you are unaware. Just do the best you can. You are human, but you have the golden thread of divinity running through your being. This is your storehouse, your powerhouse, the source on which you can call for extra strength. This is your spiritual reserve that can help you.

When others are difficult, feel sorry for them. They have missed their way. Try to win them, not with heated words but with simple truth. They will learn in time. What you are doing is the choice made by your free will, perhaps one of the most important gifts conferred on you by the Great Spirit. You could have been puppets, marionettes, with no ability to reason, think, challenge or question.

Instead you have potentially all the infinite qualities of divinity. You call them into being when you face challenge. This is the fire in which the steel is forged. This is the priceless opportunity; so show your mettle so that the gold of the spirit can emerge and exhibit its divine origin.

Never be afraid of the challenge or the fight. The combat is good for you as long as you realise you have a spiritual purpose to fulfil. I, a somewhat older soul than. yourself, encourage you to realise always that eternal, spiritual principles are your guide lines and that adhering rigidly to them you cannot fail.

Welcoming another animal welfare worker, the guide said:

I am very glad to have you here. It is a great pleasure to welcome any servants of the spirit whose lives are dedicated to the task of spreading enlightenment and teaching compassion to all forms of sentient life.

I know that this task is not an easy one, that the path is full of difficulties, but the prizes of the spirit are to be won by those who can be the most steadfast when they are confronted with obstacles. You did not choose an easy path to follow. I am not suggesting that you complain. I am merely pointing out that this is what you have chosen to do of your own free will. There are many associated with you in my world who would like you to realise, as I think you do, that those engaged in championing causes that matter are never alone.

It is a very difficult task on which you are engaged. There are so many reforms to be accomplished. But every time you succeed in ending or lessening cruelty you are helping the eternal processes of creation to be fulfilled.

I do not have to tell you that the animals in your world have rights which are as inalienable as those of the humans with whom they share the same planet. I do not have to tell you that the evolutionary law encompasses all beings; that none can be outside this operation; that the whole of life, no matter how varied its forms, moves forward together; and that every act of cruelty, whether to humans, or animals, retards the progress of the whole of life.

You must regard it as a victory when you make any progress in this important field. You know, as well as I do,. that the evolution of the human race is bound up with the evolution of all animals. Man retards his own progress when he ignores or forgets his obligations to those who serve him with devotion and fidelity, or who are placed on earth so that man can help them to progress as he does.

All the difficulties, wars, greed, selfishness, the byproducts of materialistic thinking, these cannot be abolished until man on earth expresses the divine qualities of love, affection, pity, compassion, service. These are the divine attributes with which he is endowed. Until he manifests them he is marring his unfoldment. Every act of exploitation or cruelty hinders his advancement, apart from its deleterious effect on others, be they human or animal.

A band of great souls work with you. The man you call St Francis is almost the leader. He plays a very active part in this crusading and brings the power that he has gained since coming to our world to help in all that you are trying to do.

When you meet with problems, you have to make the decisions as to how to deal with them. There is no better rule than to withdraw into the silence and allow the divinity within to point the way where you should go.

The fields in which you labour are yours for the choosing. Organisations, societies, councils, these do not matter unless they fulfil the purpose for which they were formed. Always those with knowledge of inner life, and of spiritual values, who have access to other levels of being, should try to allow themselves to be guided so that what they do is actuated by the single motive of service.

If these words, which I have been asked to say, are of any help, then I am glad to have been the instrument for conveying them. The generals who are to be in charge of battles have to be tried and tested to ensure that they will not falter.

All that has gone before is an essential part of the trials and tests to make certain that the pure gold of the spirit emerges closer to the surface and that you become increasingly aware of that inner strength, that inner refuge, that inner sanctuary which is there and on which you can draw, or to which you can retire, as occasion demands.

"Your words are exactly what I need and will be of great

*help," said the visitor. "Sometimes we don't know which
course to pursue."*

You must always do what you think is right. Be sure you
think it is right. If there is purity of motive then what follows is
always to the good. If the motive is wrong then you have only
yourself to blame. But if you fight and lose, and the motive is
right, then you can pick yourself up and fight again.

We are warriors if necessary for war to be waged. After all,
are we not engaged in one of the biggest of all wars? This is
the war against ignorance, stupidity, selfishness,' superstition,
all the forces of darkness that resist the light. It is a war against
oppression, cruelty, exploitation, needless suffering. This is a
tremendous battle that has to be won.

If you enable one form of cruelty to be abolished then
the whole of your earthly existence is worth while. It is this
needless cruelty that must be fought again and again until it is
driven from the face of your earth. Never allow yourself to be
disheartened no matter how seemingly large the oppression.
You will continue to have victories.

You may not be able to achieve in your own earthly period
all the reforms you desire, but if you achieve one, two or three
then you have justified your existence. Sometimes I wish that
those of you who are immersed in this service could see how
the animals in our world dwell in peace and harmony, with a
complete absence of fear or terror. It is indeed a heaven for
them.

Chapter Eleven

WILL UNIVERSAL PEACE REIGN?

DESPITE man's rapid and far-reaching technological advances, too often, it seems, these discoveries could result in more terrifying tools of war and destruction.

Man's inhumanity to man continues. Will it ever cease? Will peace one day reign supreme with men and women living like the spiritual brothers and sisters they are? Is killing inevitable? Can war be justified? How does the spirit world view the increasing violence?

In these vitally important areas of life, Silver Birch gives his answers. At one circle he was asked: "Have you anything to say to people who are very concerned with the way much of the world is going, the materialism, the violence, the dreadful things that are on the increase in the so-called civilised parts of the world? Have you a message of hope for these people?"

The guide told his questioner:

I would say that the will of the Great Spirit must prevail, that those who serve the causes concerned with the amelioration of man and of other creatures, those who dedicate themselves to the task of alleviating suffering, ending cruelty, helping wherever they can, should never lose heart. The great purpose will be fulfilled in your world, slowly, gradually and sometimes painfully. You get these phases of violence, discord, clashes, war, brutality, because your world is in the melting pot. So many traditional ideas have been discarded. Youth strains at the leash. There is dissatisfaction with systems which have prevailed for too long and created privileges for people who have never earned them.

In this maelstrom it is hard for those in the thick of it to see the divine purpose fulfil itself. But, nevertheless, if you turn back and look at history you will find there has been a gradual evolution. There is more kindness and tolerance while at the same time you have had outbreaks of prejudice, cruelty and oppression. This is part of the way in which the universe must work, by the clash of opposing forces so that what emerges is better for the whole.

Do not. be disheartened. The great and important fact. is that the truths and the power of the spirit have effected lodgement in so many lands and cannot be driven out. These everywhere will continue to work their benign purpose and act as a leaven on the whole. Gradually these truths and this power will continue to infiltrate, driving out the darkness, ignorance, stupidity and cruelty, and get rid of the blemishes and foulnesses that besmirch your world. There is always good ground for hope and optimism because the Great Spirit is at work the whole time.

Said a circle member, "Hence, I suppose, the message of what we call Spiritualism."

This is the reason why it was decided that this breakthrough would be achieved, and it should not be temporary, as had happened on so many occasions in your world. What should be achieved would be consolidated and become a permanent factor on earth.

"I see our world evolving in a spiral," said somebody else.

That is perfectly true. When you. are at the lowest point of the spiral it is a very horrible looking aspect, but the highest points are most encouraging. Do not despair. Those with knowledge should never despair. You have heard me say it so many times. The Great Spirit has been in control of the universe for a very long time and knows what has to be done. There is another side to the picture. The breakthrough is being achieved in many fields of labour and activity, overturning and overthrowing ideas, many of them false ideas that have existed for too long. Gradually the forces of love and goodness will overcome those of greed, and conditions will begin to improve.

The great thing is to have no fear. Fear is an obstacle which is very difficult for us to conquer. Fear is negative, fear is corrosive. Fear and worry and apprehension, these disturb the physical, mental and spiritual atmosphere around you, making it far more difficult for 'us to get close to you.

Those who know, however little, because none of us can know much about these infinite truths, should always maintain, or try to do so, a calm, quiescent, receptive, tranquil approach to every problem. The soul who knows should be filled with resolution and with confidence that there is nothing in your world stronger than the power of the spirit which makes all life possible. If there is any message I can give and repeat, it is banish fear and you will have peace within. And as you have peace within you will have peace without.

Another question was: "We have had experience of young bullies, skinheads. It makes me wonder whether it is necessary to be armed when one goes out for a walk. There is no reason why. we should allow them to knock us down for money. Should we fight back?"

It is never right that evil should be tolerated or violence encouraged. It has been said that those who take to the sword shall perish by the sword. It is your duty to protect your physical body, the only means by which the spirit can express itself on earth. You should use your reason in all matters appertaining to your earthly existence.

Of course you should protect yourself by any means that you consider are reasonable. But you should also feel sorry for these foolish, misguided young people who are unaware of what they are doing. It is a form of massemotion, a kind of hysteria born of inferiority, a self-pity that desires to draw attention to itself as the only means of making others aware of their existence.

We have no sympathy for violence, the spirit cannot work that way. The spirit. expresses itself in tranquillity, calm and peace and quiet confidence. These conditions provide a means of attunement and of abolishing the barriers between the world of matter and the world of spirit. Violence disturbs, violence erupts, violence produces a reaction on those responsible for it. No good will come out of it so far as those who perpetrate it are concerned. Violence is one of the by-products of the gospel of materialism.

It is not only the young who are violent. They get the blame in the glare of publicity. The violence is a sign of your sick society which has lost its way in the pursuit of materialistic goals of selfishness. In this morass it strives to achieve a further violence, with complete indifference to the well-being of others. And it is a violence not only displayed to humans but unfortunately to animals as well.

It is completely wrong to say that it is due to an energy that must be channelled into such negative and destructive forces as violence. People must learn to live in harmony with one another. I am reminded of those who . say that you must have the poor in your world so that you can exercise charity towards them. If you are charitable, it is because you feel it is right. You should not require the sight of a beggar to kindle this feeling. There is so much service that the young can render with the energy they possess. Unfortunately too many have not been given the right direction. But where they have, and where they are spiritually motivated, then they are a shining example to their elders. The best of youth is to be admired; the worst is a sad spectacle.

Try not to be engulfed by this gloom resulting from violence.

and terrorism. Try to rise above it, to be in the world but not of the world, to be aware of your spiritual nature, your divine potential, so that at least you become a little lighthouse of the spirit with rays that will help those seeking to find you.

Asked about war, the spirit sage said:

The Great Spirit, with infinite wisdom and love, has created earthly children and given them some free will. The Great Spirit has also arranged the whole of their minds, spirits and bodies so that they can unfold the divinity that lies within them which, in full flower, can provide infallible signposts as to how individuals should live.

The Great Spirit could have created all the earthly children as marionettes, puppets, whose actions would be strictly regulated with no power of choice, no freedom. But you cannot have free will without, at the same time, the responsibilities of your actions.

If you have the choice to do good, you also have the choice to do evil. Good and evil are opposite sides of the same coin. So are love and hate, light and dark, storm and peace. This is a polarity. Yours is the choice as to which it shall be.

So you must come back to the motive and ask: "Why do these people wage war? What is it that they seek to share in common? Or is it to gain domination over others?" You must answer these questions. It is your world. You can make it a paradise or a hell because you have the choice and the means to do so.

"I cannot, a single person cannot," was the questioner's comment.

Your world is made up of an aggregate of single units. The more single units are determined to abolish greed and rapacity and cruelty and despotism, the more they are likely to succeed as their numbers grow. Your responsibility is for your life, your actions, your words, your thoughts. Nobody will ask you to pay the price or to receive the reward for what others have done. That is the law.

It is always to the good when people pray for peace and strive to co-operate with higher beings in our world. Together they can direct power into your world to bring an end to wars, violence and all that disturbs and threatens even the civilisation in which you live.

There will be, for a long time, outbreaks of war somewhere because man has not yet learned a simple truth. All are part of one vast spiritual family. Though you may kill bodies you cannot destroy spirits. Until this knowledge is shared and put into practice through its implications by those who direct affairs in varying lands, you are bound to have outbreaks of war.

We are not responsible for man's inhumanity to man. This is cause and effect in operation. Yes, there is a better time coming for mankind. It will and must be so. This will not happen overnight when your world will be , transformed from despondency to radiant joy. It is a gradual process. As the knowledge of spiritual truth is in the possession of more and more people, their lives are lived accordingly. The systems under which they exist are contrived to enable the spirit, the mind and the body to have the experience which is necessary for "their well-being, growth and attainment.

It is the one reason why the breakthrough of what you call Spiritualism was made in the last century. This time it was part of the plan that the power of the spirit was to stay in your world, never to be driven away as was previously the case. This power will continue to enlarge its frontiers, constantly bringing an ever-growing number of people within its, radius of beneficence. Gradually what you might call the golden age, others might say the kingdom of heaven, will be achieved on earth. I will not forecast the time that, this will take. But just as physical evolution constantly is fulfilling its purpose, so on parallel lines a spiritual evolution is playing its allotted part.

Another questioner wanted to know to what extent man is allowed to kill. It brought this response:

I don't like the use of the word "allowed. Mankind is given. free will, but in a measure that is qualified and restricted. It is not an unfettered free will enabling individuals to do everything they, would like to do. The bestowal of free will is part of the divine plan so that people have the opportunity of co-operating, of living in harmony with the natural laws, the infinite processes of creation, and achieving health, understanding, realisation and fulfilment. Were it otherwise, there would be no evolution, no development.

Without free will you would have human beings who are merely puppets with no opportunities for growth and progress, and more or less acting as robots. Because man has free will, man has also the responsibility as to how it should be used.

Killing is wrong, though there are qualifications. Because you have not the power to confer life, then you should not have the power to end it. There are qualifications because there are other considerations to be met. The more you evolve spiritually the more you realise that you must act in accordance with clear principles that are based on a knowledge of spiritual realities.

Perfection will not be achieved on earth. But there is plenty of room for improvement. Earth is only one phase of life and you will have to experience many more. You have all eternity. I do not suggest you should be indifferent to earth, but it is only a part of your whole life. Certainly strive to make it a better place. It is among the lowest of the planets in the universe. It has its evolution to achieve. And evolution is also an eternal process. Perfection is never attained because the nearer you get to it the more you realise has to be achieved.

Two visitors asked Silver Birch about Communism. One

said, "We Spiritualists seem to spend a great deal of our time and energy in combating and opposing the old religions which are dying. We say nothing about the one religion-its adherents would refuse to say it's. a religion-and that is Marxism or Communism, which now commands the allegiance, at least in theory, of one-third of the human race. It is far stronger and, more powerful than any of the old religions. There, surely, is our real enemy, in so far as it preaches a purely materialistic outlook."

What do you mean by Communism?

I would define it as the political, economic and social philosophy which is based on the writings of Marx, Engels and Lenin.

If by Communism you mean true co-operation, where there is no class division, and each member of society desires to serve every other member, it does not exist in the countries which in theory practise it. Let us be clear as to what we are saying.

The root cause of all your world's troubles is materialism. You are propounding and advocating Spiritualism, the very antithesis of materialism. You are providing evidence that it is not only a theory, but a fact that spirit is the reality. You are here today, as I am, as part of a vast spirit plan conceived by the hierarchy, with the Nazarene as its leader, to ensure that the power of the spirit was not only launched into your world, but will stay there, and that no power or combination of powers on earth will drive it away.

Throughout your world spiritual bridgeheads are being established and consolidated, so that more can be built and consolidated. The power of the spirit is here to stay in your world, and to work its benign influence. Even in those countries where officially it is banned, it is still at work, and will continue. You have nothing to fear of what the morrow will bring forth. You do your best, co-operate with us, and you will see gradually the elimination of the greed that is the cancer of the world in which you live.

The other visitor, on her son's behalf, asked if Communist guides existed. It brought this response:

Let us be clear on what is being asked. I am not concerned with labels. These mean nothing to me. Your world worships labels – Communist, Socialist, Conservative, Labour, Spiritualist, Theosophist, occultist, yes and many others. It is not the label that matters. It is the goods underneath. The origin of the word Communist goes back a long time when people believed that it was right to own material things in common. This is a very good principle.

After all, is it not just that those who have too much should give some of it to those who have too little? Does not the teacher try to transfer his wisdom to students who lack it? Sharing is part of a worthwhile principle. The whole purpose of spirit return is that we should share with you, so that you learn from us and we learn from you. It says in the Bible, "The earth is the Lord's, and all that therein is."

This means that you cannot own anything in your world, itt cannot belong to you. You can have a lease on it while you dwell on earth, but it is not yours to possess for all time. The troubles in your world arise because so many people want to try and own as much of what they think is best-nobody wants the worst. As a result, greed, avarice, selfishness are enthroned and materialism becomes the new god to be worshipped.

The by-products of materialism are alas all too painfully rife in your world. Misery, squalor, starvation, malnutrition, cruelty, needless suffering, all these are the dreadful fruits of materialism. The ideal that all should share is good. Do not be frightened of a word. The early Christians tried for a time to have all things in common, and so they could be called Communists.

It is one thing to have an ideal, but it is another to try and make it a reality by methods of torture and repression and persecution and tyranny. That is the difference. So, if you like, we have Communist guides who believe that you should share all the bounty that the Great Spirit offers. I see nothing wrong with that.

Of man-made laws the guide said:

There is no chance or coincidence, because everything in the universe is regulated by natural law. I have lived longer than you. As a result I have learned to marvel at the perfection of this natural law. It is perfect because infinite intelligence is responsible for it.

You live in this land which has a reputation for the laws it has produced, many of which are regarded as a model to other countries. Yet these laws, like those produced elsewhere by human beings,. are very imperfect. They are always full of flaws. Circumstances arise for which they have not made provision. Other circumstances appear which show that they must be repealed because they no longer obtain. So you are constantly engaged in your world in making fresh laws due to their inherent imperfection.

But the Great Spirit does not have to make new laws. No circumstance has ever arisen for whichh provision has not been made. There is no form of life, be it microscopically small or majestically mighty, which operates outside the natural law.

To end this chapter I quote the guide's statement which encapsulates a vital message:

You cannot isolate man from his surroundings in your world. You have wars, violence, disturbances, needless shedding of blood, persecutions and massacres, which are all evidence of man's lack of development. If every inhabitant of your world lives according to the spiritual principles on which life is founded, you would indeed have the kingdom of heaven on earth.

Chapter Twelve

SCIENCE—VIEWED FROM BEYOND

NOT since the Victorian era when several noted scientists investigated and attested psychic phenomena, including fullform materialisation under test conditions, have spirit gifts been so rigorously placed under the scientific microscope. It is fitting to begin this chapter with a question a scientist put to Silver Birch: "I have read and have always believed that service is very important. What is also important is the occupation of gathering knowledge, namely learning. In the spirit world how is this carried out? In scientific matters of this physical world we do experiments. Does one do experiments in the spirit world, or is it by purely mental processes?"

The guide replied:

Knowledge, like the Great Spirit, is infinite; no period can be placed on it. As you progress so you fit yourself for more knowledge. You are for ever climbing a mountain, ascending one peak, only to behold another to be scaled. Knowledge, progress, development, unfoldment, advancement, all these are eternal processes.

In your physical world you experiment to see what are the results when you try "a" with "b" and so on. We have experiments which are divorced from the physical world, because we are concerned with some of the many and varying expressions of the spirit. So we are always experimenting. Let me give a simple illustration. We have coming to our world doctors who are still concerned with helping afflicted ones on earth. They have the skills which they evolved on earth. They have knowledge of the mechanism, the workings of the human body and its many reactions.

In our world they have access to a different kind of power, some of the degrees of spirit, which is life, and how it can be applied, combined with earthly knowledge, to help the sick in your world. This is a constant experimentation involving the mixture of forces.

They must not be too strong, otherwise they will harm the instrument through whom they are to be poured. They can be increased in intensity as the human channel is more receptive and can bear the higher velocity, or power, whichever word you want to use. There is the difficulty again of finding words that can adequately express what is really beyond language. So we are constantly engaged in experiments, adding to our knowledge all the time.

At later circles came these answers to questions?

The scientific picture of the universe a century ago is vastly different from the one today.

Does this mean that scientists will move away from this materialistic research to a higher level?

It will be forced on them by the logic of their own researches as they inevitably inquire into the world of the invisible and its vast untapped potential. As they develop spiritually they will realise how this tremendous force can be harnessed for good. Then they will pay increasing attention to the development of these faculties within themselves. What is without is but an expression of what is within. The life force is indivisible. You cannot cut it up into watertight compartments. The life in the atom is in essence the same life as in the human, the animal, the flower or the tree. It is all the one life with its infinite manifestations.

Have scientists come to that level of understanding?

No, but some have. Oliver Lodge is a good example of a

spiritual scientist with an awareness of states of reality existing beyond the surface.

Do you think scientists will destroy too many people and too much before they come to an awareness?

No, there is a limitation to what scientists can do. They cannot destroy the whole of your world. The natural laws will ensure the damage that can be done in your world is not so fearful as some people think. Besides, the law of the Great Spirit in the ultimate must prevail. There are no men in your world who can thwart it. They can delay, they can hinder, but they cannot override the Great Spirit.

Those of us who have some insight into the mechanics and the operation of natural law remain confident that, come what may, however foolish people in your world may be, the Great Spirit will prevail. And the Great Spirit's laws will ensure that more and more love, compassion, charity and service will be exercised in your world.

Science is not infallible. Scientists are only human beings who can make mistakes. I do not worship the god of science. The world will not come to an end, as they say, it will continue. Are you familiar with scientists' pronouncements that have been wrong?

I should explain that I have had to study this question very closely, though I am not a scientist.

Silver Birch repeated his question, "Are you familiar with scientists' pronouncements that have been wrong?"

Very many.

So there is no guarantee that any scientific pronouncement must automatically be right when it concerns the future.

In greeting a scientist from Rhodesia, the guide said:

Your footsteps have been guided so that you have been brought out of the darkness into the light. This is part of the process by which all true human development is achieved because of the law of compensation, as low as you can fall so correspondingly high can you rise. It is in darkness that you find the light, it is in sorrow that you find joy. It is when it seems that earth has nothing to offer that the spirit can begin to find itself

This is part of the polarity, the means by which the soul begins to come into its own. In the vast order of universal activity every facet of being has its ordered part to play. Storm is as essential as sunshine, darkness as light. It is in the crucible of suffering that strength is forged. It is only when extremes are reached that growth begins to be achieved.

I am not trying to talk in paradoxes, but this is how the Great Spirit, with infinite wisdom, has fashioned the laws of progress so far as humans are concerned. But it is just as true that whatever is needed is presented when the time is ripe. The difficulties, trials, tests, obstacles, these are all essential precursors to the soul being able to express its latent gifts. They provide the equivalent to the catalyst.

If you look back you can see how, in the time of what seemed the greatest difficulty, you were shown the way, your footsteps directed so that you could begin to learn how to fulfil yourself There will be opportunities for you to help others as you have been helped by people who trod a similar path before you.

This is how the divine scheme comes into action, to bring people, one by one, into possession of eternal truths that will help them to express themselves to the fullest, to serve all who come within their orbit, to deny none who seek their aid and to be sorry for those who are given the chance to achieve self-regeneration and lose it because it would seem they are not ready. So rejoice at what has been revealed to you and realise that it is only an infinitesimal fraction of what awaits you. There are tremendous spiritual treasures still to be excavated. You will have many opportunities of serving.

At another circle Silver Birch said:

We are at work the whole time, experimenting with new forms and ideas, particularly in healing, clairvoyance and trance so as to improve the quality. But we are dependent on the material you offer us. This is the measure of your free will and personal responsibility.

We will always give more than we receive from you. That is our duty, to support, to sustain and to ensure that all your fundamental, essential needs will be supplied. The rest is up to you. We require instruments who will be dedicated to serve. I've said it before, and I will repeat, service is the coin of the spirit. To serve is noble because in service you are expressing the divinity within you.

What we ask you to do is to raise your standards as high as you can. We will always work to get you to advance slowly but surely towards the goal of achievement. What we say to you is very simple. Do the best you can, and together we will be able to help those who come to us.

Chapter Thirteen

SPIRIT CELEBRATIONS DESCRIBED

THOUGH Christmas and Easter are primarily religious festivals, they have become increasingly tarnished by materialism and lost their basic lustre. In this illuminating and inspiring address, Silver Birch describes how these events are celebrated in the Beyond. His words go far beyond the relevance of these festivals and anticipate the time when "love, compassion, mercy and responsibility will guide man ... The wolf will lie down with the lamb because there will be peace on earth."

It is a practice among those of us who belong to certain groups to retire to the inner spheres at two festivals which long pre-date your Christian counterparts, Christmas and Easter. These, as you know, have their origin in the celebrations in ancient times of the passage of the sun as it appeared to those who saw in its appearance, its lengthening and shortening, the symbols of divine activity.

When the sun attained its full glory it was regarded as the period of resurrection, when nature sang its paean of praise and displayed its profound beauty for all to see. That which had been sown was reaped in its splendour of growth.

Correspondingly there was the winter solstice when, after the high noon of summer, there came the drooping as nature prepared and husbanded itself, fertilising and making ready all growth which had to appear when the cycle had achieved completion.

So at Christmas you had the birth of the sun, the end of the long cycle when there arose the first sign that new life was being born into your earthly world.

Those times had a significance to us because it was then that we received the greatest communion from the Great Spirit. You do not yet understand very much the influence of the sun. At these times, we held for many days what you call seances. We received at those festivals much inspiration.

So, when it comes again to the time which all of us regarded as the most important in our lives, we gather together and celebrate with those who are our own. This started with the influence of the sun, but that was only a symbol. There is an influence from all life to other life, from all matter to other matter, and from all planets to other planets. This time is chosen because all of us are associated with races whose religions were founded upon the laws of nature. To us, the festival of the birth of the sun was the greatest of all because it represented the beginning of a new era. It is the end of the cycle, and a new one begins.

Because these festivals were held in the world of matter, they are celebrated in the world of spirit. A spiritual meaning has now come out of them. Instead of celebrating the dawn of the new life, we now use it to withdraw from the world of matter to get new power of the spirit so that we can bring new light to your world.

And because those of us who are associated in this task belong to more ancient races than your western civilisation, we utilise these festivals as opportunities for withdrawing to the inner spheres where we belong. We take counsel, we share experiences, we learn how far we have succeeded or failed. New plans are discussed. We meet those who sent us on our mission.

Among them is the great figure of the Nazarene, who is still imbued with the task of teaching humanity the age-old truth enshrined in all that we seek to do, that love is the fulfilling of the law. I wish that you could see and hear the Nazarene and feel that great love as he encourages us in our missions, as he expresses his knowledge of all that has been done and urges us to go forward with new strength, with new hope, with new vision and with new purpose. He is not the Nazarene of the Churches, exalted into a deified place, but a great spirit who strives still to serve through many instruments.

For a short time I am in the spheres where I now belong, to feel once again that vitalising power of the spirit, so invigorating in its strength, so 'beautiful in all its fulness, making you realise what life is when you are able to experience it in the higher realms of the spirit. I speak with all humility and with no pride at all.

If all the beautiful paintings of the world, all the inspired visions and all the great artistry that you have ever heard of in your world of matter, and all the deepest and greatest beauties of nature were all combined into one whole object, it would be but a very pale reflection of life in the higher regions. When the artist is filled with inspiration he realises that it cannot be expressed with his few pigments, and he longs for the colours that could be blended to produce that richness that has been given to his soul. But there is none, for spiritual truth and beauty exceed material clothing.

How can I describe spiritual exaltation in words? How can I describe the joy of meeting beings who radiate the great light of the Great Spirit, who are full of wisdom and understanding, mercy and tenderness, who know all before you convey it, who are aware of your innermost thoughts, who see the workings of your mind, who know of your successes and failures?

The great message of love, which has characterised all religions, and which was epitomised in the teaching of the

Nazarene, is still the one we proclaim in the name of the Great Spirit who is the lord of all life, the infinite creator.

Thus, returned to our true spiritual state, we experience some of the lustre, joy, radiance, beauty, richness, nobility and grandeur which are our natural environment. We bathe in it, rejoice in it and capture the glories that, were our normal expression. That is our celebration.

Then, counselled, enthused, refreshed, invigorated, recharged and revived, we return to your cold, grey, dank, clammy, dark world to continue the task of piercing its fogs and mists, striving to shine through with the light of truth which can guide and point the way for many weary travellers.

Some of the spirit of -love is expressed in your world at this Christmas time. It takes the form of geniality and generosity, the desire to give. It is to be seen in the remembering of old friends, the cementing of old ties, the bringing together of those who have been parted and the resolution to forget old enmities.

Alas that it should be preceded by the great holocaust and bloodshed, when so many needless sacrifices are made of some of the Great Spirit's dumb creatures. What a pity that the birthday of the "Prince of Peace" is commemorated by such a dreadful slaughter; the blood of innocent creatures has to flow in order to commemorate peace. This is the crucifixion of your world, celebrating peace by making war on innocent creatures.

One day, love, compassion, mercy and responsibility will guide man who has dominion over the lesser creation which looks to him for help. When these qualities are expressed in human life, bloodshed, cruelty and needless horrible experiments which are wreaked on these innocent creatures will cease. The wolf will lie down with the-lamb because there will be peace on earth.

Chapter Fourteen

TO INSPIRE "AMBASSADORS"

*FOR most of the delegates at this large meeting of the
Commonwealth of churches connected with the Spiritualist
Association of Great Britain, held in its Belgrave Square
headquarters, it was their first chance of hearing Silver Birch.
He readily accepted the invitation to address them.*

After a typical invocation he told them:

I am very happy to come amongst you and to bring you my
love and greetings from the world of spirit. I would like you
to feel that we are not strangers to one another, but that we are
comrades actuated by the same motive of helping wherever
we can and playing our part to bring. spiritual, mental and
physical freedom to all who come within our orbit.

I would also like to say just a few words which perhaps may
be of some encouragement to all of you who are channels,
instruments, dispensers of the power of the spirit which
produces in its train such vivifying effects.

Then I would like you to appreciate that none of you is ever
alone, overlooked, neglected or forgotten. You have made
yourselves accessible to the sublime power of the spirit, which
is the mightiest force in the boundless universe. It is the power
of life itself. That is why, for example, in your healings you
are able to obtain results where other means have failed. You
enable the life force to produce its rejuvenating effect on the
life force of the sufferer you are helping.

You are all privileged to be ambassadors of the Great Spirit.
You are representatives of the Great Spirit wherever you labour.

It becomes your charge and responsibility to see that your gifts are used in such a fashion that they produce the maximum good wherever you can.

There will be brought to you those whom you can help. They will often be pitiful derelicts, sick, ill, worried, cheerless, full of problems, feeling that life on earth has nothing more to offer them. It becomes your privilege to help them to become aware of themselves, of their true nature, of their inner spirit, the gift of divinity conferred at birth, so that they begin to get a realisation of how they should order their lives and derive from them the fulness, richness, beauty, splendour and radiance that should be theirs.

That is your function, to make the power of the spirit available to all who come to you. It is the reason why you have buildings, churches, temples and societies, so that you are accessible. And accessibility is the reason for the existence of all your organisations.

I want you to appreciate that so far as we are concerned, if you help only one soul to find itself, to become aware of its latent divinity and to begin to express it, then the whole of your earth life is well worth while. But you will be able to help more than one. You will be able, as a result, to perform this unique service that no others in your world can possibly give because they have made themselves inaccessible to the power of the spirit which is the life-giving essence for the whole cosmos in which we all dwell.

Do not worry if any come to you and after you have done your best you are unable to help them. They have had their chance. You must be sorry because they have not taken it. What you must realise is that until their soul is touched, until they are spiritually ready, there is nothing you can do to help them.

What will produce this preparation is not always easy to understand. It may be an illness. It may be a crisis. It may be anything which brings them to the lowest depths of despair, when they feel there is nothing in the whole of the material world that can produce the answer. Then they should begin to come into their own and you should be able to kindle the divine spark so that it can begin to grow into a lambent flame. That is why you exist in your churches, societies and organisations.

I must also say this. Because of what you are, because this tremendous power, divine in origin, flows through you, yours is the greater responsibility to see that you do nothing that in any way lessens the trust that is reposed in you. We are not dictators. We are not your masters. We do not regard you as marionettes who have to dance when the strings are pulled in our world. You are our co-operators. We want to work together. We will always provide whatever is spiritually necessary according to the conditions available at the time.

We will lead. We will guide. We will direct. We will help, but we will not order. We will not compel and we will not dictate. If you hear, supposedly emanating from our life, entities who command you to do this, that and the other, you can be sure that their spiritual status is not very evolved. Co-operation is the law of the spirit. We would win you with love, with common sense and with reason. We would offer you nothing that is an insult to your intelligence or would make your reason revolt. Together we can help the Great Spirit in the eternal processes of evolution and creation.

This is the task on which we are all engaged. This is the opportunity given to all of us to help,the Great Spirit so that His children may live a richer, fuller life and not waste all the opportunities earth provides in obtaining the equipment that is necessary when people come to our side of being.

We get too many misfits, too many ill-equipped, too many derelicts who are unready. It is easier for their education to begin in your world than it is in ours. So be aware of the tremendous possibilities that lie within you. Be aware of the great opportunities that you have for service. Do the best you can and then you will be fulfilling the purpose for which you came into your world.

Two years later the guide addressed the Council of Spiritualists, which was then composed of the Greater World Association of Gt Britain, Spiritualists' National Union and the Union of Spiritualist Mediums. Among his comments were:

Wherever there are human beings there are difficulties and problems, because you are imperfect beings living in an imperfect world. If you were perfect you would not be on earth. You would have joined the apex of divinity which is the great spirit of life.

You must expect troubles, difficulties, problems, pitfalls and differences of opinion because you are very human. But if you have compassion, if you are prepared to cooperate, to be democratic, to sink self and let the good of the many prevail, then you will come through. And we will always help you. The trouble is that there are too many people-I am not referring to your council-who are more concerned with themselves than with others. These are the stumbling-blocks in the promulgation of any truth.

We are always on the look-out for means of ensuring that spirit truths and power should advance in increasing measure. We bring together, wherever we can, those who can help to ensure that the spirit plan goes forward. It is not an easy task because the manipulation of matter from our world is very difficult and involves many problems. We have to work with very delicate and subtle vibrations which can be easily nullified by foolish actions in your world.

If you will co-operate with us, and forgive my saying this because I mean it most kindly, not demand, but be prepared to receive you will find that in this atmosphere we can accomplish much together. It is always desirable to have unity in diversity, but not to try to achieve uniformity. You can unite on the fundamentals on which you all agree. There must always be differences of opinion because all the individuals within the ranks of what you might loosely call the Spiritualist movement are at different stages of spiritual and mental growth and evolution. They cannot think alike.

Some of you are perhaps already familiar with the fact that you have discarded views, beliefs and opinions that you held dearly in years gone by because a greater understanding has brought you a different perspective. And so the great necessity is for toleration. Brotherhood does not mean that you all agree. It means that you recognise brotherhood in spite of your diversities. That is the only way I can put it. You must try to achieve the ideal. You may not succeed in doing so 100 per cent.

Go on trying to enlist others, because co-operation is part of the law governing the universe. You should always. strive to achieve it among yourselves. After all, basically you are agreed on the prime facts. There are differences of interpretation. Respect one another's viewpoints and combine on what you can agree. This is not easy. But I always say that generals must not expect to be given easy battles to fight.

Chapter Fifteen

POINTS TO PONDER

EVEN those who are convinced of Survival and Spiritualism's philosophy, which gives life new vistas and broadens horizons, can get depressed, despondent and downhearted. These "Points to Ponder" are taken at random from Silver Birch's teachings. Their purpose is to uplift and encourage.

Do not worry about the morrow, today is all that matters. Discharge to the best of your ability the duties you are called on to perform. Do your best, that is all we ask of you. You are human. If you were not weak you could not know what is strength.

Truth is simple yet paradoxical. In darkness you find light, in sorrow you find joy, in crisis you learn to find peace. Hold your heads high. There is nothing that can obstruct what it is you have to do unless you choose to turn aside from the path that lies in front of you.

The signposts are provided to point the way. When mists obscure them, pause. Because they are mists they will roll away and destiny will show the path to be followed. The sun shines even when clouds obscure it.

These things I teach because of what I have seen. So I rest my confidence in the Great Spirit and its infinite power. This cannot fail. We, with our defects, weaknesses and blemishes can fail, but failure is also a means of learning the lesson of how to succeed.

Life is not a monotone, neither is it inertia. Nature abhors a vacuum. Life is motion, radiation, vibration. There must always be movement, mostly forward, occasionally backward. The worst thing is to stand still.

You will have reverses, but they will enable you to appreciate the greater victories as they come. Learn to withdraw from the clangour and strident noises produced by your world's cacophony. Learn to allow inner peace to flood the whole of your being.

The soul is most active in peace, stillness, quietude, receptivity, attunement. Often you achieve far more spiritual activity when asleep than when awake. This is when strength and guidance come to you.

Our function is to show the way that leads to spiritual mastery, to the full flowering of the gifts with which you have been divinely endowed, so that those who are brought to you can be helped to find themselves and to know, as you do, the purpose of being and how to order their existence so that, they derive from it the beauty and richness which should be theirs. All is going well. There is no need for depression or despair. We are on the winning, not the losing, side. The forces of reaction are in disarray. They cannot out-manoeuvre infinite wisdom when it seeks to make its mark on receptive souls.

The tough jobs, are for the tough people. It is no good giving them easy tasks. It is an index of attainment that the harder missions are assigned to those competent to perform them. The generals in the great war against ignorance and superstition must have been tried in the battlefield before, otherwise they will be incapable of exercising generalship. So, paradoxical as it may seem, the tougher the task means the greater the achievement that has made it possible.

You will have problems. That is why you are on earth, to overcome them and in doing so finding new strength, greater developments. Welcome every problem as a challenge to be met, and to be beaten every time.

*   *   *

The Great Spirit has so ordained life in your world that you will find strength when you think you have reached the limits of weakness. It is when people seem at the end of their tether, and that nowhere can they find in the material world anything to help them, that they are ready to be illumined by the truths of the spirit.

*   *   *

You cannot escape the problems of earthly life. They are inevitable, the stepping-stones you must encounter. But as you weather the storm so you are spiritually stronger as a result and helping to shape your character into a higher mould. It is the difficulty that enables you to achieve spiritual strength and growth, so do not be afraid of it. Just regard it as a challenge to be met and to be conquered with the power that you have within and the power that you can call on from without.

The great thing when you have this knowledge is never allow shadows in earthly life to appear so strong that you are engulfed in darkness. They are only shadows; they are not reality. The reality is the spirit. The spirit is the divine within you. The spirit is what gives you life. The spirit is the most potent force that you have within you and within your reach as well.

I know you are all human and so must fall by the wayside. But if only you could.pause and remember as the shadows come closer that they cannot obscure the real light which is the light of the spirit, then you can be radiant, unmoved and strong in your complete confidence that you must come through. It is a hard lesson to learn.

If it were easy it would not be worth while. You cannot have it both ways. If you want mastery you have to discipline yourself And if it were too easy you would not fulfil yourself

Daily life in your world is a challenge to be accepted and, whatever its nature, to triumph over. If you allow the spirit to express itself then nothing can stand in the way.

It sounds easy, but it happens to be true as well. I do not make the laws. I can only tell you how they operate. Each morn when you awake is the herald of a new day with possibilities for greater spiritual equipment. Greet it so that when the day ends you can feel you have helped your spiritual growth, that your stature has increased and that as a result you are better equipped for what the morrow will bring.

* * *

Do not allow yourselves to be downcast no matter what the problems that come to you in your daily lives.

We cannot promise a bed of roses, an easy path with all the stones removed. What we can promise is that if you fulfil yourselves spiritually you will be the better for it. As a result, you will have justified the reason for incarnating into the world of matter.

Every problem is a challenge to be met and to be overcome. In the process your spirit grows, develops, unfolds and more and more of latent divinity rises to the surface. Do not express gratitude when things are easy, but when they are hard. Those are the tests that you must face and in facing them you emerge spiritually stronger as a result. You must be sorry for those who surrender. If they have awareness and have seen the light, then it is a greater pity that they have given in. It is for us the saddest spectacle of all when those who have knowledge behave not in accordance with what they know to be true.

* * *

We are all human. If we were perfect we would not be where we are. Perfection, or its attainment, is an infinite process. It is not possible in your world to have all-knowledge. Knowledge is infinite. The conditions under which you live provide restrictions on what you can receive and assimilate.

The plan is that in the darkest hour, when the world of matter seemingly has no opportunities to point the way, knowledge is given to you, first through evidence that life, because it is spirit, is a continuing process. Then you become, the recipient of that divine beneficial power which enables you to heal the afflictions of those who call on you.

These provide the foundation on which you have to build your faith. We do not decry faith, provided it is reasonable and not credulous. The belief in that which is unreasonable is an insult to the intelligence which is one of the divine gifts that have been bestowed on every one of the Great Spirit's children.

Those you love and who love you may be separated from you physically, but spiritually you are as united as you always have been. Love is stronger than death. Love, like the spirit, is among the most important forces in the whole universe.

It is not possible for us to prevent you from encountering the storms and troubles of earthly life. Neither can we shield you when you are buffeted by them. Occasionally we have to leave you to your own devices to see how you fare when trials beset you and there are lessons to be learned.

You must have the comparison, sunshine and storm, to appreciate the realities of your existence. After all, what is hate but love inverted and subverted from its true purpose? This is a matter of soul development.

It is in darkness that you find the light; it is in storm that you find peace; it is in sorrow that you find joy because life is a paradox and a polarity. You cannot appreciate health until you have suffered. You cannot appreciate sunshine until you have endured the rains. Suffering is the catalyst, the divine means by which a soul can come into its own and realise he or she is not only a body but an eternal spirit using it. That spirit is the divinity within, the spark which spiritual healing should kindle so that it can grow into a radiant flame. And that is the purpose behind all spiritual healing.

The universe is subject to evolution. It is an evolving universe. Perfection is not achieved anywhere. It is an infinite process. Every stage of purification, which eliminates dross, makes you realise there is still more dross to be eliminated. You are on an eternal path to perfection which you will never attain. Therefore there must be inequalities for the time being. There must be the rough edges, problems and difficulties, all caused by the law of evolution outworking itself.

* * *

You must live for the day, for the hour, for the minute, for the second. Have no anxiety for the morrow and do the best you can. The Great Spirit is aware of the fact that you are all very human beings and imperfect. This is why you are on earth. If you were perfect you would not be where you are now. The function of your earthly life is simply to eliminate the imperfections.

* * *

Do the honest best you can. Exercise the tolerance and charity which. are the hall-marks of the evolving spirit. None of you is perfect. You will not necessarily agree with one another. Sometimes, because you are human and imperfect you will make mistakes because your opinions will be wrong. Therefore toleration, charity, receptivity and love are the qualities that should be expressed. If the desire to serve is right, the means will be forthcoming. You will not be abandoned. You will not be left entirely to your own resources. You will always be helped, whatever emergency arises.

If you do not like troubles, and I do not blame you because this is a human failing, then you cannot expect to grow spiritually. Growth comes only by meeting trouble, accepting the challenge and overcoming it. In any effort to serve, and in your case to serve those who are helpless and cannot serve themselves, you have a host of evolved beings by your side. They will not fail you. You will triumph, not easily, not without difficulty, not without trouble, but you will come through. The power of the spirit never surrenders. It always triumphs.

*   *   *

Your world is full of difficulties and problems. It is a sad world, a drear and violent world in which too many have lost their sense of values and their priorities. There is a great war raging between the forces of good and darkness. It is on instruments like you and others that we rely to stand fast and firm when the challenges come, to meet them by calling on the powers within that you possess and even greater powers that are at your disposal, and to triumph over every obstacle and handicap that comes your way.

In the many years in which I have been privileged to serve you, I have seen that however dark the shadows loom, they prove to be only shadows obscuring temporarily the eternal sun that is always there. I will continue, with others close to you, to do my best to ensure that if you do your best, we will see that everything you need is provided for you.

If only the people of your world, especially those who have

the knowledge of spiritual realities, could see beyond the senses of matter and realise what is round and about them, they would never worry.

*   *   *

Matter is an obstacle; matter is heavy, leaden, dull. Spirit is light, delicate, sensitive. You have to use five physical senses through which the divine spirit can express itself. It is like the violinist who has a poor instrument on which to play. He has within his soul the most. inspired music, but the instrument is restricted and cannot convey it. Your bodies are dull clods of earth. Yet these are the only means through which the spirit can express itself.

There are times when, apart from your personal conditions, the atmosphere surrounding you, and the earth on which you live, are full of hatred and violence which does not make it easy for the spirit to penetrate. This mass of obstacles surrounding your world presents a very grim picture when we approach it.

*   *   *

So far as we are concerned, we wish to transform the world in which you live, from the wretched, dark, miserable, fearful, violent, sick world that it is, where greed dominates, where selfishness rules, and where all the spiritual attributes are expressed only by a minority.

It is part of our work to ensure, as far as we can, that we will not only spread knowledge of eternal spiritual realities on which all life is based, because life is spirit and spirit is life, but also to teach, whoever is ready to listen, that they are spirits with bodies and not bodies with spirits, that the body is merely the temporary house through which the owner is expressing himself.

*   *   *

The difficulty is that you in your world would like us to produce the results in your way and in your time. But we cannot do that. We can only do it in our way and in our time. Because our vision is more extended, I think it is true to say that we are the better judges of what is best for you. The worst thing that could happen to a lot of people would be if their prayers were answered.

*   *   *

The Great Spirit has no physical hands other than those which you provide. You are the tools for the operation of spirit power in your world. Be open, be receptive, try to clear your minds of preconceived ideas. Be imbued with a desire to serve. In, that spirit you will attract all the help that is necessary for the service you have to render.

*   *   *

Keep radiant, optimistic and cheerful. Try never to allow yourself to be downcast. The best atmosphere in which we can work, help and guide is one in which there is no gloom, no despondency, no despair. All these blanket the aura and create obstacles that have to be surmounted.

Punishment and reward are both due to what you inflict on yourselves. You make your own punishment. You make your own reward. This is cause and effect, sowing and reaping. The sequence is immutable.

It is never a bed of roses for those who have to serve. Even the most beautiful roses have thorns. In the attainment of spiritual mastery the road to be travelled is a hard one., As you walk along it so gradually familiar landmarks have to be left behind.

*   *   *

The greater the mission that is to be performed the greater are the challenges that will be met. It cannot be any other way. More is expected from those who have the gifts of the spirit, the perception to understand their implications, than others who do not possess these talents and are unaware of anything in your world except its surface.

*   *   *

I do not have to tell you and others that we always render service for service and that those who serve are not overlooked. I cannot always convey it to you in the fashion that you would like, but we strive to instruct you so that it is conveyed to you in the fashion that you would prefer for your sake. It is better to raise you to our level than for us to come down to yours. This, after all, is the whole object of what we try to teach and the ideals we strive to inspire in you and others so that they can fulfil themselves.

I know it is not an easy path, but the captains in the army of the spirit must not expect things to go easily for them. More is required from ones who have the knowledge than from those who are completely ignorant -of what the spirit has to offer them.

You are the repositories of the greatest power in the universe. It is the power of the spirit. There is nothing or nobody that can burke that power, that can overthrow it, that can prevent it from fulfilling itself. You must always remember that if at the end of your earthly lives you have succeeded in helping one soul to find itself, then your existence has not been in vain.

*   *   *

If you have this knowledge and fail to live up to it, then you must pay the price because ignorance is not your excuse. Knowledge inevitably brings responsibility. More is expected of you when you have truth. And this is the great trust that is reposed in you.

It is my constant theme that knowledge brings responsibility. You cannot have all the benefits of knowledge without having at the same time the responsibility of what you do with it. That is your free will, and the measure of your responsibility which none other than yourself can fulfil.

The natural laws of the Great Spirit ensure that divine justice is ultimately meted out. None can escape the natural law. Provision has been made for you, and for every manifestation of being in your world and in other worlds. The law is supreme. The law overlooks none. The law ensures that all you need for your spiritual growth and development will be available when you are ready to receive it.

Motive is the acid test. You cannot cheat the law. The millionaire who gives money to charity does not increase his spiritual growth by doing so. But the one who gives what he cannot afford because he knows it will help, his stature will increase.

Compassion is one of the attributes of the spirit. I've said it so many times. Love, affection, friendship, compassion, mercy, tolerance, kindness, service, are the attributes of the spirit. When you express them you are manifesting yourselves spiritually.

*   *   *

There is nothing in the world of matter that can quell your spirit. Your spirit is greater than anything that appertains to the physical body. When things and people seem difficult sometimes, withdraw into the silence. Allow the great love emanating from our world to enfold you in its embrace and to recharge you with its power, so that you emerge stronger as a result.

* * *

You have to be fluid in your outlook. Fluidity is the only way to approach matters of the spirit. Dogmatism leads to sterility. You must have the open mind. The power of the spirit is infinite; therefore it is limitless. What you have achieved in your world is merely scratching the surface of the vast range of spiritual treasures awaiting you.

We do not dictate. We do not regard you as puppets or marionettes to be manipulated. We desire to co-operate so that you develop your receptivity to become greater instruments for the power of the spirit, whether it be in the form of inspiration, communication, healing, or any aspect of mediumship. There is room for all.

* * *

At some stage in every individual's earthly life there comes a moment when the soul is ready to receive. This is the opportunity the Great Spirit affords every one of His children. Sometimes it has to be achieved through sickness, bereavement or crisis. But this is the catalyst which enables the soul to unfold.

Spread knowledge wherever you can. Remember, you are the emissaries of a power greater than anything to be found in your world. That is. not only a privilege but a responsibility. Never behave in any way that would diminish the love and respect in which you are held.

Strive to be tolerant, compassionate, sympathetic, humane,

wherever you can. If others misjudge you, regret it for their sake. If you can help, extend a hand. Serve whenever you can. These are simple but profound truths. Go your way, do your work the best you can. This is all that is expected of you.

*   *   *

Always remember if you meet with rebuffs or harsh criticism, not to worry about it. It means that would have had their chance and are not ready. You must be sorry for them. The Great Spirit has so ordained it that throughout earthly life, every individual is given a chance of coming to grips with spirit truths, the foundation of life.

You must strike the right balance. You must ensure that at least equal attention is given to the things of the spirit as is given to the things of matter. What I can say, without fear of contradiction, is that no spiritual enterprise, sincerely, reverently and humbly conducted, will fail for the lack of means to ensure its success.

*   *   *

Try always to remember the eternal principles upon which life is founded and to live in harmony with them. That is the way to ensure the tranquillity, repose, calmness, peace and inner stillness that must come to all those who are in tune with the larger aspects of being.

*   *   *

Once you have achieved spiritual awareness you create a magnetic link with the larger life and its denizens. You are always held within their embrace to ensure the maximum of protection at all times. Hold on to that which has been revealed and let that be the foundation. Know there is nothing in the world of matter that can destroy that foundation. Rest the whole of the days that are to come on that basis and face them fearlessly in that knowledge because there is nothing to fear in your world.

*   *   *

There is no happening that can destroy the soul. Every circumstance is a means, however difficult it may be, of enabling the soul to achieve even greater growth. It is not easy when you are in your world, surrounded by all its problems and difficulties. Remember there is a scale of eternal values. They are spiritual realities. To these you must always cling whenever doubts assail you, as they will always do. Do not excuse your weakness because you are human, but realise that weakness can be transmuted into strength.

*   *   *

Worry is a bad counsellor. Worry and fear are your foes, not your friends. Resolution, calmness, confidence, determination, these are the attributes of the soul that knows. You have been guided, you will be guided. When there are doubts, pause, withdraw and let the spirit show the way. In this great battle all officers must be able to stand at their posts untroubled when the conflict rages. To do so they must have been tried and tested. Hold your head high.

*   *   *

Fear is the worst enemy. Fear corrodes. Fear impedes the channel through which help can come. Fear disturbs the physical, mental and spiritual atmosphere around you. Fear is the enemy of reason. Fear prevents that calmness of outlook and resolution of mind which are your greatest allies in your life.

So always cast out fear as the shadow that has no real substance. Besides, light is always stronger than darkness, knowledge is superior to ignorance, truth must vanquish superstition and come into its own.

*   *   *

The philosophy we are trying to instil is that you live for the moment. Never fear what the morrow will bring. You have knowledge. Use it. Let that be the base on which you build the whole of your outlook.

We say that you should have the confidence born of knowledge, that pessimism should never play a part in your earthly lives. You should always welcome the morrow as the harbinger of a wondrous adventure and possibility that it has for you. Your life should be exhilarating. Cast out fear. Fear is a product of ignorance and superstition. We are privileged to live in the sunlight of knowledge.

*   *   *

Gird up your loins. You are engaged in the great battle against greed, selfishness, cupidity, stupidity and all the horrible results of the materialism that causes trouble, disaster, war, strife and hatred in your world. You have a great work to do. Do it in the realisation that the power behind you is mightier than all the forces that the world of matter can muster. You have nothing to fear at all.

*   *   *

Life is paradoxical; life is always positive and negative; action and reaction. It is only through the interplay of seemingly opposing forces that are part of a fundamental unity that progress is achieved.

* * *

There is no such thing as luck. There is only the law. Nothing happens by chance. In a law-governed universe everything is regulated cause and effect.

* * *

You must do whatever you think is right and whatever your conscience gives the direction. You are in the end your own judges and will be able to assess, when looking back, whether the things you did were always right or sometimes wrong. If the motive is to serve, it cannot be wrong. Motive is the paramount consideration.

Look neither to the left, nor the right, nor backwards. It is a mistake to look backwards. The pages of the past are closed. They cannot be opened. It is today that matters. The future will result from what you do today.

Chapter Sixteen

SILVER BIRCH PRAYS

EVERY session of Hannen Swaffer's home circle begins with an invocation by the guide, who is responsible for hundreds of them. Their themes are common, but no two are ever exactly the same. Here is a characteristic prayer by Silver Birch:

Oh Great White Spirit, throughout all ages, in visions, in trances and in dreams, seers have beheld glimpses of the supernal realms beyond earth and have come to realise something of Thy infinite majesty and Thy divine splendour. In fitful bursts of revelation they proclaimed truths of the spirit, the eternal, inflexible, inexorable laws by which the whole of the universe is governed.

Now we are engaged in the same task, striving to spread truth about Thee, to disabuse the minds of all Thy children of the many slanders on Thee. Thou hast been depicted with wrath, jealousy, vengeance and partisanship as the inevitable accompaniments of Thy deity. We strive to picture Thee as Thou truly art, the infinite intelligence behind the natural law which rules with love, wisdom and beneficence.

We draw attention to Thy divine attributes which are resident within every human being. And we strive to teach them how to order their lives that Thy divinity may find its fullest expression. Thus shall they become aware of Thee, of themselves and of their loved ones and comrades in the higher realms who seek to use them as the instruments of Thy dispensation.

We desire to draw all mankind together in bonds of love and fellowship, that they may co-operate more closely and purge their world of all the evils that are the outcome of selfishness, greed and avarice. In their place we would have a kingdom founded upon a knowledge of Thy laws.

When that is achieved man will live in peace; all the arts will flourish and love will abound; goodness, tolerance and sympathy will be expressed by all; many cancers which disfigure the world will have been banished and light will reign everywhere.

This is the prayer of Thy Indian servant who seeks to serve.

COMPLETE YOUR COLLECTION

All of Silver Birch's books make superb reading, providing inspiration, illumination and perhaps occasionally consolation. Over the years, the guide answered literally thousands of questions on almost every subject imaginable. The complete list of available Silver Birch titles is shown below. These can be read and enjoyed either individually or as a complete set, one which makes a unique collection to refer to time and time again. Each volume gives the guide's views on a comprehensive range of topics both here and hereafter.

The Silver Birch Book of Questions and Answers
Compiled by Stan A. Ballard and Roger Green. This latest Silver Birch title is in easy-to-read question-and-answer form. It answers literally hundreds of points, such as. "Do we reincarnate on earth?", "What are the spiritual aspects of heart transplant surgery?" and "Can euthanasia ever be right?"
240 pages. £7.99

The Seed of Truth
Compiled by Tony Ortzen. Based upon two earlier out-of-print titles *Silver Birch Speaks* and *More Wisdom of Silver Birch* which were compiled by the medium's wife, Sylvia. It contains an account of when actress Mary Pickford, "the world's sweetheart," met and questioned Silver Birch. Each chapter ends with one of the guide's uplifting prayers.
174 pages. £7.50

Lift Up Your Hearts
Compiled by Tony Ortzen. This carefully chosen selection of teaching comprises the guide's wise words over a twenty-year period. Animals, a spirit view of death, mediumship and karma are just four of the many subjects explained. Features a verbatim account of when Doris Stokes and Doris Collins, two of Britain's most famous mediums, were addressed by Silver Birch. 229 pages. £7.50

Philosophy of Silver Birch
Edited by Stella Storm. A former secretary to Maurice Barbanell and then chief reporter at *Psychic News*, Stella Storm covers such issues as natural law, lessons of bereavement, the responsibility of mediumship and "Healing, the greatest gift of all." Silver Birch also tells what he would say to a television audience. This popular book is now in its sixth impression. 155 pages. £7.50

More Philosophy of Silver Birch
Compiled by Tony Ortzen. In easy to read question-and-answer form, of special interest are two chapters which trace man from birth to what lies Beyond. Social problems, reincarnation and science are amongst other subjects examined. This title ends with inspiring bite-sized "points to ponder."
253 pages. £7.50

Silver Birch Companion
Edited by Tony Ortzen. Drawing upon *More Teachings of Silver Birch* and *Wisdom of Silver Birch*, this volume features an account of the night Maurice Barbanell died and the days that followed. Features the replies the guide gave to a Fleet Street editor.
159 pages. £7.50

A Voice in the Wilderness
Edited by Tony Ortzen. Most of the material in this book came from handpicked cuttings at the archives of *Psychic News*, though it also draws upon the out-of-print *Home Circle* and *Spirit Guidance*. Read the advice the guide gave to a Member of Parliament, a senior Army chaplain and delegates at an International Spiritualist Federation congress.
128 pages. £7.50

The Spirit Speaks
Compiled by Tony Ortzen. An abridged amalgamation not only of *Silver Birch Speaks Again* and *Anthology of Silver Birch* but also important teachings that originally appeared in *Psychic News*. Amongst its highlights is a word-for-word report of a meeting betwen Silver Birch and film star Merle Oberon, who was devastated when her fiancé was killed in a plane crash.   142 pages. £7.50

Guidance from Silver Birch
Edited by Anne Dooley. A former Fleet Street journalist, Anne Dooley later became a reporter at *Psychic News*, first 'meeting' Silver Birch in 1963. Amongst subjects in this compilation are the problems of suffering and communication with the spirit world.   120 pages. £7.50

Teachings of Silver Birch
Edited by A.W.Austen. First published in 1938, this classic Silver Birch title has so far run to seven impressions. It contains a fascinating Foreword by famous journalist Hannen Swaffer, after whom the Silver Birch circle was named. Silver Birch tells his own story and, as usual, answers countless questions, including life in the spirit realms.   243 pages. £7.50

Silver Birch Anthology
Edited by William Naylor. Love's supreme power, what happens after we die and "Who is Silver Birch?" are just three of the topics in this absorbing book. Originally published in 1955, the philosophy within this book is still fresh, vital and valuable.   132 pages. £7.50.

Light from Silver Birch
Compiled by Pam Riva. Contains the last ever teachings from Silver Birch after the sudden passing of his medium Maurice Barbanell on July 17th, 1981. Also featured is Maurice Barbanell's obituary, which, ever the keen journalist, he prepared in advance. His mission with Silver Birch lasted sixty-one years. Pam Riva was the medium's secretary at *Psychic News*, the paper he founded in 1932.
218 pages. £7.50

The Universe of Silver Birch
By Frank Newman. This book is unique as Frank Newman has examined Silver Birch's teachings and measured them side by side with the deductions of modern science. This brings important new insights into Silver Birch's philosophy. The result is an intriguing, thought-provoking volume.
118 pages. £7.50

...

Silver Birch Speaks   Now you can hear the guide in the comfort of your own home. This sixty-minute cassette was recorded at a special sitting, during which a selection of questions was put to the guide.
£4.95 (plus postage and packing)

Silver Birch Meditation Print After Silver Birch was painted by psychic artist Marcel Poncin, the oil portrait had pride of place in Maurice Barbanell's London flat. Now it is available as a full colour A5-size card. The reverse contains an inspiring message from Silver Birch.
£1.65 (plus postage and packing)

How to order:

Please send your order to Psychic Press (1995) Ltd., The Coach House, Stansted Hall, Stansted, Essex CM24 8UD. Telephone 01279 817050. The cost of postage and packing will be advised upon receipt of order. Credit card orders can be taken by post or telephone or faxed on 01279 817051 or e-mailed to pn@snu.org.uk

Please make cheques or postal orders payable to

Psychic Press (1995) Ltd.

Only sterling cheques can be accepted.